PSYCHOSYNTHESIS OF THE COUPLE

Roberto Assagioli, MD

Men and Women in Relationships

*Presenting for the First Time in English
A Composite Essay Synthesizing His Lectures*

Edited with an Introduction
by Jan Kuniholm

With a Reminiscence by Piero Ferrucci

CHESHIRE CAT BOOKS

Writings and Notes by Roberto Assagioli
copyright © by Istituto di psicosintesi, Florence, Italy
Translated and used by permission

An Uncommon Couple by Piero Ferrucci
Copyright © 2022 by Piero Ferrucci
Used by permission

All Translations and other essays
Copyright © 2022 by Jan Kuniholm

All Rights Reserved. No part of this publication may be reproduced, distributed, or transmitted in any form or by any means, including photocopying, recording, or other electronic or mechanical methods, without prior written permission of the author or the publisher, except in the case of brief quotations embodied in reviews and certain non-commercial uses permitted by the U.S. Copyright Act of 1976.

Front Cover Credits: upper left photo by Wolfgang Hasselman on Unsplash; upper right 1960 photo of Roberto and Nella Assagioli courtesy of Isabelle Clotilde Küng; lower left photo by Caleb Ekeroth on Unsplash; lower right photo by Magdalena Kula Manchee on Unsplash.

Back Cover Credits: upper left photo by Nick Fewings on Unsplash; upper right photo by Sara Dubler on Unsplash; lower left photo by Wynand van Poortvliet on Unsplash; lower right photo by Wade Lambert on Unsplash.

Published by
Cheshire Cat Books

P.O. Box 599
Cheshire, MA 01225-599 USA
www.Cheshire-Cat-Books.com

ISBN 978-0-9882024-4-3

ACKNOWLEDGMENTS

I would like to thank everyone who has participated or assisted in the creation of this book. My thanks go out to Isabelle Clotilde Küng in Switzerland for alerting me about the existence of some of the documents used in the creation of the Composite Essay, and for generously providing me with scanned copies of original documents she had obtained directly from Roberto Assagioli in the 1970s. Thanks also to the Directors and staff of *Istituto di psicosintesi* and the Assagioli Archives in Florence, Italy, who provided assistance in tracking down documents used to create the Essay and gave permission to translate and use them along with notes, photos and diagrams from these articles and elsewhere in the Archives. Thanks to Catherine Ann Lombard for her contributions to the translations from the Italian. I also wish to thank Walter Polt and Kenneth Sørensen and especially Douglas Russell for their feedback and generous editorial assistance. Thanks to Piero Ferrucci for allowing me to use his lovely reminiscence of Roberto Assagioli. Thanks especially to my wife, Bonney, who has supported me in this process and encouraged me in so much — my life as half of a couple is inextricably linked with her, so in a sense this is her work as well as mine. Our life together provided the impetus for this work.

—Cheshire, Massachusetts, June 2022

PREFACE

What happens in a relationship between a man and a woman? Does something special happen in the best, or most developed, of these relationships? Are there some things we can learn about them that will help us and other people in our relationships?

The relationship between women and men is at the fulcrum point of the entirety of the human race — we all emerge from such relationships in one way or another — and yet our human history is littered with the trauma and wreckage left by relationships that were "sad, mad or bad" in one way or another, and that left indelible marks upon succeeding generations. In our own time the situation is not improving to any noticeable degree: domestic violence, addictions, and divorce are only a few of the signs that tell us that troubled relationships are ubiquitous in our culture. They have deep and far-reaching effects in a way that perhaps no other relationships have.

Late in his life, Italian teacher and psychiatrist Roberto Assagioli, MD (1888-1974) wrote that "the crisis in the relations between the sexes ... can perhaps be said to be the outstanding aspect of the general crisis which is deeply affecting the very foundations of existing civilization." This book is intended to provide a small contribution toward meeting that crisis.

At the core of this book is a composite essay drawn from numerous essays, lectures, and interviews that Assagioli gave on the topics of marriage and couples from 1957 to 1974. His framework for understanding human nature and development is called "psychosynthesis," and he was recognized as a gifted and insightful therapist as well as a wise student of human nature, whose work and thought was recognized internationally. He worked to provide insight into healthy human lives and relationships. Recent research has discovered that the Division of Psychotherapy of the American Psychological Association voted to present Assagioli the 1970 award in their annual Great Therapists Series. The award was declined only because Assagioli was unable to travel to the United States in fulfillment of the conditions of the award.

We believe that Assagioli's thought on relationships, marriage, couples, and what he called "inter-individual psychosynthesis" provides continuing inspiration for contemporary students of human nature as well as practical insights for therapists and for people who wish to enrich their lives and develop their relationships with those closest to them. If the relationships between men and women are in crisis, putting Assagioli's insight and wisdom into practice for ourselves, our families and our clients may provide one of the ways of addressing this crisis.

CONTENTS

Acknowledgements   iii
Preface   iv

Synthesizing Roberto Assagioli by Jan Kuniholm
    Assagioli's World in Time   1
    Women as Partners in Assagioli's Life   3
    Assagioli's World in Language: Science and Poetry   4
    Masculine and Feminine Principles   15
    Synthesizing Roberto Assagioli   17

Psychosynthesis of the Couple: by Roberto Assagioli, MD
Compiled and Edited with Notes by Jan Kuniholm   20
    A Couple: The Smallest Psychological Group   23
    Complexity and Multiplicity in Every Human Being   25
    Differential Psychology of Men and Women   27
    Stages of Union   34
    Higher Perspectives   43
    Mutual Respect and Ideal Images   47
    Various Types and Degrees of Psychosynthesis
       I. Extent or Amount of Communication   49
       II. Levels of Communication   49
       Differences in Intensity   50
    Reason for Difficulties   51
    Elimination of Obstacles   51
    Pathology of the Couple   52
    Love, Attraction, and Synthesis   58
    Ways to Agreement and Synthesis   66
    Reference Sources   75
    Additional Bibliography   77

Appendix A: Selected quotations from
"The Balancing and Synthesis of The Opposites"
by Roberto Assagioli, M.D.   78

Appendix B: "Yin and Yang"   80

Appendix C:
Quotations from "Gender in Chinese Philosophy"
in *Internet Encyclopedia of Philosophy*   81

An Uncommon Couple:
Memories of Nella and Roberto Assagioli
A Reminiscence by Piero Ferrucci   82

Index   85
About the Authors   90

Documents, Photographs, and Diagrams:

Archival documents and the Assagioli essays used as reference sources are taken from the Assagioli Archive, Florence Italy, and used by permission. Photographs are of unknown origin and are public domain, having been used by numerous writers for decades; all diagrams have been duplicated from Assagioli's originals by the editor, except for the one titled "I" Moves Toward Identification with Self, which was created by the editor.

Roberto and Nella Assagioli, with son Ilario, c. 1923	3
Hand-Written Note Archive Document #877	22
"Egg Diagram" Map of Human Being	26
Scheme of Man's and Woman's Bio-psychical Characteristics	29
Relationships at Various Levels	32
Stages of Union	34-35
Hand-Written Note Archive Document #15763	37
"I" Moves Toward Identification with Self	44
Hand-Written Note Archive Document #15607	45
Various Types and Degrees of Psychosynthesis	49
Love as a Mission	59
Hand-Written Note Archive Document #8565	67
Roberto and Nella Assagioli c. 1970	82

SYNTHESIZING ROBERTO ASSAGIOLI
Jan Kuniholm

We are pleased to present a new composite essay compiled from writings from various lectures and essays by Roberto Assagioli, MD, titled "Psychosynthesis of the Couple." We were fortunate to discover and gather writings and transcripts of lectures and talks that Assagioli presented from 1957 through 1974 on the topics of "psychosynthesis of the couple," "psychosynthesis in marriage," "the human couple," "inter-individual psychosynthesis," and "a higher view of the man-woman problem." I discovered while in the process of pursuing different research, and their discovery presented a unique opportunity to present new material to an English-speaking audience. Some of the originals are in Italian or French, and material from these are translated and presented in English here for the first time. The remainder of the originals are in English, but to our knowledge have mostly not been previously published or widely known. Assagioli's talks and writings discussed these related topics several times over the years, and it is clear that at different times he emphasized different aspects of the issues presented here; his perceptions and experiences in these final decades of his life prompted him to revise some of his thinking. It is for this reason, and to avoid duplication of material that appeared in multiple sources, that we present here an essay that is a selection of materials from many documents. This portion of Assagioli's thought is generally new to most of us who are native English speakers.

Assagioli's World in Time

Roberto Assagioli, MD (1888-1974), the founder of psychosynthesis, lived through a time of immense change in Europe. This was a time when the western industrial civilization, with all its attendant benefits and drawbacks, began to accelerate in Europe. The new science of psychology was finding a place in medicine and science. Assagioli was one of the first Italians to study the psychoanalysis developed by Sigmund Freud (1856-1939), although he departed from the Freudian community and many of the Freudian viewpoints after completing his doctoral dissertation. He was a colleague of C.G. Jung (1875-1961) and Alphonse Maeder (1882-1971) who also left the Freudian camp to develop their own approaches to psychology, and whose thought had a significant influence on Assagioli. He was drafted into the Italian military during World War I and served as a doctor on the Austrian front, although little is known of his activities during or immediately after the war. But then he lived through the rise of Fascism in Italy, its eventual alignment with Nazism in Germany, and the disaster of the Second World War, from which he barely escaped with his life. Assagioli worked as a doctor and psychotherapist from the time his early war service ended until the end of his life. His own approach to understanding the human being, "psychosynthesis," was an attempt to include the higher as well as the lower aspects of human nature in the study and treatment of people, focusing on the whole person and not only on pathology. Certainly his work was equally devoted to both women and men, and we have discovered some of his writings that are focused on the relationship between the sexes.

Psychosynthesis has long been associated with "conscious evolution," and its founder was able to provide an outstanding example of this approach in his own life. Quite late in his life he was confronted with a society — a world, even — in which attitudes and thoughts concerning women and families were changing radically. Those changes have continued into the present. He himself came to adulthood in a post-Victorian era that was marked by a severe "conservatism" in these areas; and in his native Italy the social dominance of men, especially under the rule of the Italian monarchy (which remained in Italy until 1946), was such that women did not achieve the full right to vote and participate in political life until after the end of World War II. The Fascist government (1922-1945) did what it could to enforce a "traditional" view of women and families, even mobilizing government propaganda to urge women to bear children, but surprisingly the Fascists were among the most ardent supporters of women's full participation in society — in theory. One of the regime's spokespersons even said, "The fascist state can't conceive of a woman locked in her house."[1] The regime liberalized laws and created women's sports, which had been entirely absent in Italian life prior to 1922. Nevertheless, "ideas about the appropriate social behavior of women have traditionally had a very strong impact on the state institutions, and it has long been held that a woman's 'honor' is more important than her well-being."[2] Assagioli emerged from this culture presenting a radically different view of people than was generally accepted in his country — and in most of the western world — at the time.

Women as Partners in Assagioli's Life

It can be instructive to recall that women were among the strongest influences in Assagioli's life, and that his approach to "the human couple" was manifested in his marriage to Nella Ciapetti. As Catherine Ann Lombard has written, "as his second wife, [Nella] always seems to appear either as a footnote in his biographies or as a complex and fragile character in the margins of his activities." But she was in fact very involved with his work: as Lombard shows from one of Assagioli's notes, he was careful to never make a major decision alone, for his own intuition for the right response could easily lead him to make mistakes.[3] So Nella was probably involved, in some way, in much or all of his work from their marriage

Roberto and Nella Assagioli, with son Ilario, c.1923

---

[1] https://en.wikipedia.org/wiki/Women_in_Italy accessed December 2019.
[2] Ibid.
[3] Lombard, Catherine Ann, "From the Couple to Humanity," in *A Wild and Free Creature*. Lulu. 2019.

in 1922 nearly until her death in 1973, and one can easily surmise that it was by mutual agreement as well as accepted custom that only his name would appear with the work of the *Istituto di Psicosintesi* and in his writings. Nella in fact had been an active published author and organizer of theosophical events, and co-hosted the meetings that eventually resulted in the creation of the Institute of Psychosynthesis. Paola Giovetti, in her book *Roberto Assagioli – The Life and Work of the Founder of Psychosynthesis,* reports that Nella organized and managed the activities of the Assagioli properties and the family business.

In a section titled "Women's Psycho-Spiritual Gifts" in her book, *A Wild and Free Creature,* Catherine Ann Lombard provides some insights into the women who inspired and influenced Assagioli. Among them was the Contessa Gabriella Spalletti Rasponi, who was in fact the first president of the Psychosynthesis Institute in Rome, to whom Assagioli said the Institute was indebted for "her moral and material support."

These insights provide some of the background for understanding Assagioli's approach to "the psychosynthesis of the couple," for he did not regard women as appendages of men or as second-class human beings. We will see that he describes a process of development that engages two full partners.

Assagioli's World in Language: Science and Poetry

Assagioli wanted psychosynthesis to be viewed as a science, and he had a great respect for the sciences. On the other hand, he had little use for what some people now refer to as "scientism," which is a narrowed-down, skewed version of scientific work and scholarship that has become so pre-eminent in our contemporary world. Assagioli wanted "evidence-based" science to be the basis of psychosynthesis, however in our time the term "evidence-based" has come to exclude all work that does not conform to a particular rigid orthodoxy of theory and practice. One of the areas that this orthodoxy is enforced in modern scientific work is in its use of language.

Assagioli came from a tradition that thought of "science" together with the terms "learning" and "experience" in such a way that the objective was always to discover knowledge and understanding, especially knowledge that can usefully be applied in real life. Unfortunately, the philosophical doctrines of logical positivism infected the major scientific disciplines early in the 20th century. Positivism's mania for logical and linguistic precision, exactitude, and consistency became the driving force in moving "evidence-based science" into a corner where only experiments involving statistically significant populations in double-blind verified measurements became truly acceptable. This means that mountains of legitimate work — based on valid evidence, but not meeting these narrow standards — goes unrecognized, unpublished, or is dismissed as "anecdotal evidence." Psychosynthesis approaches its subject in the broadest meaning of the word "science," in which clinical experience and personal results are favored over reports based solely upon data. Personal results are unique to each person and are usually not subject to quantification, but are nonetheless significant.

Roberto Assagioli was a true "scientist of the spirit," as he has been called, but he was also a "poet of the soul." It is important for us to understand that his language can be, at times, as much the language of a poet as that of a scientist. It is relevant to know that he combined these roles in perceiving a step-by-step process of psychological growth and development in Dante's *Divine Comedy*, which was a continuing inspiration for him, and that he saw clear scientific principles at work in Patanjali's *Yoga Sutras*. Yet he was also well informed and conversant concerning much of the current scientific thought of Europe and North America throughout his life. For him, there was no loss of meaning, clarity or force when language was used with breadth and nuance. But this means that readers of his work are required to do some work of their own to extract the maximum benefit and learning from his words. And we sometimes need to parse his words carefully in order to discern the context in which he spoke, because he addressed himself to specific people at specific times and places. This is consistent with psychosynthesis itself, which focuses on the individual as the foundation of all other work with larger groups and populations. It is not a discipline that can be mastered without personal as well as scientific involvement: He was known to have said words to the effect that students who came to study with him in Florence who "would not do the work" would have to leave. "Doing the work" meant not only studying psychosynthesis "objectively" but living it and applying it to themselves in their own lives. In this sense, then, psychosynthesis is like many older, established sciences in which the pioneering investigator begins his inquiry with himself as the subject before moving on to study and teach others.

The use of language is important in our modern reading of the "synthetic" essay on "psychosynthesis of the couple" that follows. He sometimes uses words in a way that a modern reader may take amiss if they are taken, shall we say, "too literally," or with the assumption that the language is being used only in the very precise way that a modern positivist scientist might require. Assagioli was giving live talks to students, visitors, and people he knew, and his focus was usually on practical and clinical application more than on "theory." So when he used the word "man" he might mean, "all men," or "some men," or "most of the men whom I have seen in my practice over the years," or "one man whom I am addressing specifically at this moment." In a live talk, the discussion following his lecture could help clarify things in a way that a reader of a printed essay may not appreciate or benefit from. As modern readers it is important for us to weigh a word within its verbal context, and within the larger context of the entire teaching and practice of psychosynthesis. And it is important to keep in mind that Assagioli was not primarily a writer: the most complete and accurate versions of his teaching were transmitted *in person*. Much of his writing that we now have includes transcriptions and adaptations from talks and live events. If what we take Assagioli's words to mean does not fit within the context of the overall text and psychosynthesis as a whole, we are probably mistaking his meaning. If we try to shoehorn his language into a positivistic level of definition and precision, we will easily miss the truth in what he is conveying.

Some words in particular were commonly employed in Assagioli's talks and writing, that may cause some confusion or misinterpretation, particularly for readers who do not have a thorough understanding of psychosynthesis. The language was used because he was addressing people within the context of psychosynthesis, and some understanding of it is needed to follow him with full understanding. We'll look at some examples: the words "identification" and "higher," and the verb "to dominate."

The first word, "identification," is a technical term in psychosynthesis. It describes a common process that may occur on several different levels of a person's life, at different stages in the process of growth. It may denote something that is an obstacle to personal growth and maturity, or something that indicates great personal progress. Identification has to do with what or who "I am." We may not even use the words, but there may be a sense or a feeling — such as " I am so stupid!" or " I am a good mother" or "I am very strong" in the sense that the quality *is* myself in some way. When we "identify" with a subpersonality, we have equated our personal self, the one who looks in the mirror and says "**I** am here, that's **my** face," with a small portion of our being such as the collection of qualities and behaviors that we employ when we are doing our professional job, or being a housewife, or being a student — that is, with only a *part* of ourselves. We are mistaking the part for the whole and saying (usually unconsciously) that "I am" . . . that part. One way to describe what happens in such a partial identification is that our self, the observer, mistakenly confuses itself, the observer, with what is being observed. Assagioli presented an exercise, a procedure, to help guide people into releasing such partial identifications — a "disidentification exercise" that is a vital tool in the process of personal psychosynthesis.[4] With this exercise we realize that we mistakenly say "I *am* . . . (something)" when in fact we can learn to distinguish the *self*, the observer, from that "something" that is being experienced, felt, thought, or observed. On the other hand, when our personal self "identifies" with our higher or

---

[4] This exercise is found in many publications, and is discussed in detail on pages 103-111 of Assagioli's book *Psychosynthesis: A Collection of Basic Writings*, published by The Synthesis Center, Amherst MA, 2000.

spiritual Self, then the one we call "I" is aligning with the greatest perspective and range of abilities that are possible for us — a *whole* identification. So in psychosynthesis, "identification" is when we connect with our sense of ourselves, our "I."

Our second example, a term that Assagioli uses frequently and that gives some people (including some longtime students of psychosynthesis) trouble, is the word "higher." Assagioli's overall map of the psyche is divided into three sections, labeled "lower unconscious," "middle unconscious," and "higher unconscious," as will be seen in the diagram on page 26 in the following essay.[5] Assagioli also uses the word "higher" in other contexts, and it usually refers metaphorically to a specific dimension of being human, often associated with "higher" thoughts, feelings, purposes and so on — often taken to mean "more developed," or "more advanced," or associated with constructive meaningful values in some way.

In modern energy psychology, "higher" and "lower" literally refer to energy frequencies of both sound and light, and although Assagioli's sources in this respect were traditional, modern studies are confirming that the words "higher" and "lower" are not used metaphorically in energy work.[6] In many traditional studies and disciplines the "lower" frequencies are associated with "dark," destructive, or more limited thoughts, feelings, impulses or actions; or with aspects of the body, moving "up" in frequency through the organs and glands that are associated with "light" or other "higher" emotional, mental and spiritual processes to the "higher" frequencies that are associated with mind

---

[5] Assagioli emphasized in a lecture that "unconscious" is an *adjective*, not a noun. Even though we may say "the unconscious" in an unguarded moment, he explains that this refers to portions of our experience of which we are not presently aware, or hold in our waking focus.

[6] On the other hand, other terms such as "light" and "dark" are sometimes used literally and sometimes metaphorically in such work, and it is important not to confuse such usages. The metaphorical use is almost always based upon the important literal experience of *light* as supplying life-supporting energy, and should never be taken otherwise. Any transference of such usage into moral or racial judgments is a misuse of the term.

and purely "spiritual" processes.[7] Some contemporary studies and practices in energy medicine are confirming the presence of different energy frequencies in the human system, and developing new means to work with them.[8] The "Higher Self," (or just Self with a capital S) for Assagioli, is the transpersonal core of our being, residing partly in our higher unconscious, having access and communion with other Selves and with Universal Self; it is the Source of our personal selves and its energy radiates into all aspects of our normal lives (including our bodies), usually without our conscious awareness. Bio-energetically, the Higher Self is associated with the crown (highest) chakra in the body, which in yoga is considered to be the entry point of universal energies into the body. Exploring this connection is beyond the scope of this essay, but it is helpful to keep in mind that Assagioli uses the word "higher" in both metaphorical and literal senses at various times.

Assagioli worked with energies in his practice and was fully committed to his understanding that the progress toward maturity in a person was also the path from focus on "lower" energies toward that of "higher" energies, and that the "higher Self," sometimes called "spiritual Self" or simply "Self," is the repository of a person's *highest* energies, broadest and deepest perspectives, most profound knowledge and inspiration. There

---

[7] In Ayurvedic medicine and many forms of modern energy work, the energy intake center or *chakra* that is lowest to the ground on the body, the first chakra, is associated with the color red; moving upward through the body the successive *chakras* are associated with orange, yellow, green, blue, indigo, and violet — successively higher wavelengths — as the energy approaches the crown (the *highest* point) of the head. Many energy workers observe these colors in their practice and some have found that the application of the color of light associated with its related *chakra* is therapeutic. Also energy workers use successively higher sound frequencies on the *solfeggio* scale for therapeutic work on each chakra — lower frequencies are helpful for "lower" *chakras,* and higher frequencies are helpful for higher *chakras.*

[8] Examples of modern energy workers and teachers include Barbara Ann Brennan and Donna Eden, whose many works are available online and in print, and who both have developed extensive educational programs to train practitioners worldwide. Their work can be used in full congruence with psychosynthesis.

have been students of psychosynthesis who have associated the word "higher" with hierarchical politics and abusive dominating behavior (as in "higher up the corporate ladder" or "higher up the political pyramid"), or who have not agreed with Assagioli about the personal energies moving in the direction of transcendence, arguing that the "immanent" energies are equally vital and important in the life of a person. This is not the place to deal with such discussions, although it is this writer's observation that Assagioli's emphasis on the transcendent never excluded what is immanent. The two are interwoven in human existence.[9] His approach was one of fitting the approach to the situation, one might say — and he was fully cognizant that energies flow both "up" and "down" the human system. However, it is important for us to get a sense of what Roberto Assagioli himself meant in his use of the word "higher," which he associated with particular energies, abilities and perspectives. He wrote a short essay called "Psychological Mountain Climbing" to emphasize that getting to a "higher" place, physically and psychologically, is partly a matter of gaining perspective and ability to act, as well as the development toward identification of the personal self with the Higher Self, which has access to a greater range of awareness, activity and being — and energy. And again, it is important that we understand his use of terms in both "scientific" and "poetic" senses, for us to extract the fullest range of meaning and practical value from what he says. It is important that we not allow a contemporary positivistic narrowing of meaning for words to retroactively confine Assagioli's vision.[10]

---

[9] In *Psychosynthesis*, page 182, Assagioli wrote, "The individual is never absolutely alone and God (or the spiritual reality) is never purely transcendent, but always in living relationship with the manifestation. This is not the same thing as saying that the relationship IS the reality." In *The Act of Will*, (2010 The Synthesis Center, page 69) he wrote of "Universal Being or Beingness: The Supreme Value, Cosmic Mind, Supreme Reality, both transcendent and immanent." So for Assagioli, transcendence always included immanence. In his book *Transpersonal Development*, (page 77, 2007 edition) he makes the relationship explicit.

[10] It is also important that we realize that some later writers, such as John Firman and Ann Gila, have disavowed the concept of "higher Self" entirely in their "revision" of psychosynthesis. This changed focus and structure created a different approach which was not in accord with Roberto Assagioli's experience or teaching, which are reflected in the present set of essays.

The third example is a term that appears in the following essay, one that Assagioli returned to repeatedly: the verb "to dominate." The use of this word with reference to individuals and to members of a couple often makes sensitive people cringe. Roberto Assagioli's career as a psychotherapist spanned decades, and the reality of what he witnessed in people included the tendency of many people of both sexes and of all ages to assert themselves, to "want what they want" in such a way that they ignore or override the thoughts, feelings or desires of other people: the tendency to *dominate* others.[11] This tendency includes controlling behavior that may be overt and "extroverted," or covert and "introverted." He did not hesitate to name what he witnessed. He clearly saw that behaviors of one person dominating another person were generally harmful, and stated clearly that *the* single greatest obstacle to harmonious relationship was *excessive self-assertion*. Doubtless he saw it in all its many manifestations, and also saw that it so easily tips into *dominance*. Power over others can be a playground for abuse, and people in a committed relationship do, he said, need to yield half of the authority in their lives to the partner in their relationship. The risk of dominance is very real in many relationships. It is important to keep a clear-eyed vision of such possibilities, and Assagioli keeps it in focus.

It is worthy to note that Assagioli also used the word "dominate" in a positive sense when he taught people how to detach themselves from the limiting identifications (in connection with his "disidentification" exercise cited above), and the use of this word has again caused sensitive people to step back. But it is again important to see Assagioli's language in all its potential in both scientific and poetic senses. When a person exercises "dominance" within oneself, it can be applied in a "tyrannical" manner, but most beneficially it is a term to denote the effort to gain

---

[11] In this, Assagioli was completely in step with more modern researchers who have uncovered what are asserted to be biological tendencies in people toward exerting dominance over others, particularly in men. The term, as he uses it, is only tangentially related to *political* dominance, but the term arouses an emotional reaction in those who have a justified fear of fascism and political coercion.

healthy *control* and *mastery* over one's own life, to forge an inner harmony that requires a degree of effort, of assertion — of will — to accomplish. Assagioli's favorite metaphor for the ideal use of the will in psychosynthesis was the conductor of an orchestra, who directs, organizes, interprets, but does not *coerce*. But in the following essay, devoted to relationships between couples, the dominance that Assagioli observed was usually behavior that was not benign, and is not constructive when it becomes unbalanced. He clearly saw that members of a couple need to learn to modulate and alternate their assertive tendencies, and urged people to learn what was required to allow them to live together.

Another term that Assagioli uses with some frequency is "function," which he uses in two quite separate contexts, with different meanings. First we find that he refers to roles and behaviors with this term, "function," in a way that suggests that he is generally talking or writing about functions as "what we do." It is important that we understand that he did not intend that this word should imply rigid or unchangeable behavior. Assagioli explicitly does not accept Aristotelian "either-or" logic: he points out that, for example, there are "functions" that need to be fulfilled in a family for the benefit of the children; however, he does not specify precisely what those functions "must" be or who "must" discharge them, or how. He insisted that "each one of us, man or woman, has roles and functions to fulfill, individually, inter-individually and socially. Here is where the differences begin. These are most emphatically not differences in value, only differences in function."[12] His own evolution is made evident when we read in one of his 1965 lectures that he felt the need to delineate a polarity of "paternal" and "maternal" functions in the family; but by 1972 he recognized that most of such functions were not polarities, but necessary activities that are capable of being met by either parent. Then in other contexts, the word "function" is used in the sense of a "channel," "extension," or "means of expression," to refer to the expression of the Self

---

[12] Assagioli, Roberto, and Claude Servan-Schreiber, "A Higher View of the Man-Woman Problem," first published in the journal *Synthesis*, in 1977.

through the personality in what are generally called the "psychological functions" of sensation, emotion/feeling, impulse/desire, thought, imagination, and intuition, which interact spontaneously or as directed by the will. However we need to be alert that at other times and places Assagioli has referred to these "functions" as "levels," as discussed below.

Lastly, it seems necessary to discuss the fact that Assagioli's fluid use of terminology (or perhaps, at times, an imperfect grasp of the English language) in the selections that follow — which, we must remember, were delivered orally or written for different audiences, in different languages, at different times — results in some terms being used in what occasionally may appear to be ambiguous ways; or the same terms being used in alternative manners. For example, in discussing the "egg" diagram of the structure of the human being (page 26), he describes the three main "levels" of our being: lower, middle and higher unconscious. At another place he refers to four "fields" or "levels" of life: the physical, the emotional, the mental, and the intuitive. Then at another place he refers to the "soul level" and the "personal level," which seems to be analogous to other writings in which he refers to the "physical level" and the "spiritual level." Yet in the larger context of his work, the "four levels" bear some similarity to the four psychological functions developed by C.G. Jung, but toward the end of his life, particularly in his book *The Act of Will*, Assagioli said that his experience required him to expand the list of psychological functions to seven: sensation, emotion/feeling, impulse/desire, thought, intuition, imagination, and will. Assagioli's delineation of seven psychological types, to be used to aid in understanding some aspects of personality, seems to be closely aligned to these seven functions. These functions appear to have some overlap with what Assagioli calls "the four levels," which were probably an earlier formulation in which the level of "intuition" served as a bridge function between the personal or physical level and the soul or spiritual level. It seems clear that the formulations of Assagioli's thinking, if not its essential conceptions, changed over time and continued to evolve right up to the end of his life.

In the diagram called "Scheme of Man's and Woman's Bio-psychical Characteristics" in the following composite essay (page 29), we find the four "levels" — physical, emotional, mental, and intuitive — described as "spheres of life." This diagram was used in two different presentations: first a talk given in English at a psychosynthesis conference in the USA in 1958, and second in the fifth in a series of lectures given in Italian in Florence in 1965, so it is apparent that he kept this outlook as his thought evolved. In this diagram, Assagioli attempted to schematize a few of the prevailing polarities that he observed between men and women, and it appears that the "spheres of life" are general approaches to aspects of human living that overlap the "levels," and "functions" in both of the senses discussed above. The purpose of this diagram was not to pigeonhole the sexes, but rather to illustrate how the personal styles, emphases, and some default behaviors of men and women, as he had observed them over decades, can be seen to be often contrasted. In his 1974 interview with Servan-Schreiber he emphasized that he had no intention of using such concepts to rigidly define "masculine" and "feminine" roles, but only to point out some common tendencies that are often encountered. It turns out that scientific research since 1974 has largely confirmed his observations, as will be discussed in a future book by this writer.

The "bottom line" is that we need to approach Assagioli's words in the context in which they were presented, and to realize that they are an attempt to communicate realities that are not easily reducible to simple categories. It is important for the reader to get "a feel" for what words mean in a particular context, and to refrain from insisting that psychosynthesis, or its founder, can be ordered into a logically precise, finished, system: he expected psychosynthesis to grow, to mature. The realities that psychosynthesis describes and which it helps us to navigate are seldom, if ever, neat categories or linear progressions. Psychosynthesis is at home in the quantum-fractal universe, and must be approached with flexibility and nuanced interpretation for us to extract the meanings and significance — and the practical benefits — to be found in it.

Masculine and Feminine Principles

Roberto Assagioli made reference to a "masculine principle" and a "feminine principle" in numerous writings and notes, some of which will be represented in the following essay. However, he never defined what precisely he meant by these terms, and he suggested that we eschew any attempt at precise definitions in this area. He was not writing only of people, but of people as manifestations of larger forces that actually exist. By refusing to *define* these terms, Assagioli is, on the one hand, counting on our having a general understanding of what is meant by them; on the other hand, he wants to make sure that we do not fall into a rigid typology of men and women based upon these principles. This is a particularly sensitive issue in our culture at this time in our history. For over two thousand years political, sociological and personal pressures, attitudes and behavior that have included outright violence, have been exerted in Western culture and it has had the intent and effect of denying rights, aspirations, freedoms, and behaviors — mostly of women — in the name of "natural principles." We commonly call this abusive phenomenon "sexism." But that misuse only occurs when there can be true, proper and correct use; so it is still necessary to inquire whether there are, in fact, such principles, regardless of whether they have been invoked wrongly or to enforce abuse or oppression.

In returning to our "general understanding," then, what then can we say about a "masculine principle" and a "feminine principle?" In the Assagioli Archives we find notes that give us clues as to what Assagioli meant by these terms. His note in Doc. #8061 reads, "Will and imagination. Will = masculine principle, initiative, fecundation. Imagination = feminine principle, elaboration, working out." In Archive Doc. #11096 his note reads, "Fundamental bynary [sic] division Masculine and Feminine Principles and consequent corresponding types."

Other writers have also referred to a common assessment of "masculine" and "feminine" qualities. One good example is by Rachel Naomi Remen, MD, in her book *The Masculine Principle,*

The Feminine Principle, and Humanistic Medicine.[13] When Assagioli presents his diagram of "Man's and Woman's Bio-psychical characteristics" (see page 29) he taps into a common perception of men tending to be more mentally or intellectually oriented and physically active and energetic, and women tending to be more intuitive and emotionally oriented. But these are qualities of expression, not bedrock principles, and therefore Assagioli is careful to indicate that even in the common "caricature" of the sexes, these qualities are almost never without admixture of their opposites.

In order to provide some context for Assagioli's understanding of what he called "masculine" and "feminine" principles, we are including at the end of the Assagioli essay some quotations from his own essay on "Balancing and Synthesis of the Opposites" and two selections dealing with the Chinese terms "yin" and "yang" which provide some perceptions that are analogous to the way Assagioli sees these principles.

It is clear that Assagioli shares one approach to the union of the sexes with a variety of other writers and thinkers of his time, especially philosopher Hermann Keyserling (1880-1946) and psychiatrist Alphonse Maeder (1881-1960). The highest or deepest core of the human being is beyond this polarity of the sexes, and the work (the "objective") of a couple often is to "become more like each other" in a way — becoming balanced in the expression of qualities. What he and other writers and researchers have emphasized is that one cannot work to synthesize qualities and polarities unless one first recognizes their existence.

Some political movements of the 20th and 21st centuries in particular have often adopted a blindness to the differences between the sexes in order to correct social and political inequalities and injustices. Short-term gains have been made by these tactics, but as contemporary researchers are showing, the confusion between "social equality" and "sameness" is resulting in a long-term loss of opportunities for many people.

---

[13] San Francisco, Institute for the Study of Humanistic Medicine, 1975.

It is for this reason that we are deliberately including Assagioli's writing concerning the differences between the sexes, and between masculine and feminine principles, while some of our colleagues have held that his thinking in this regard is "out of date." Assagioli did keep current with social changes, and was quite aware of the changing relationships between men and women that were already becoming pronounced in his time and which have continued into our own era. But he also refused to relinquish his anchor in what is timeless. His objective in psychosynthesis was to provide pathways for human development, and a necessary step in all development is recognition of existing conditions and recognition of underlying timeless realities.

Synthesizing Roberto Assagioli

The essay that follows is an attempt to distill or synthesize Roberto Assagioli's teaching with regard to couples. His work was clearly too encyclopedic and broad for us to expect that we have captured the essence of his thought in a few pages. And of course, even the essays we have used for sources do not represent his "complete" thinking on the subject. Eleven different works have been used to create this essay, including some published essays and some unpublished lectures and talks given to students in Italy and the United States. Assagioli's thinking concerning the couple clearly evolved from 1957, the date of the earliest source document, to 1974, the year of the latest. During that time tumultuous social changes were in progress in Europe and North America, particularly those changes marked by what is generally called "the women's movement" — the drive among women, supported sometimes by men, to secure freedom of behavior, expression and choice — as well as legitimacy and recognition — in a variety of contexts.

But other changes were also occurring that were significant to Assagioli's work. He read widely, and kept himself informed concerning developments in academic and clinical psychology, social movements, and spiritual developments. He was one of the founders of the field of Transpersonal Psychology and contributed to the early issues of both the *Journal of Transpersonal Psychology* and *Journal of Humanistic Psychology*. He was instrumental in the founding of Meditation Mount in California, of the School for Esoteric Studies which is now in North Carolina, and participated in numerous conferences focusing on psychosynthesis and other disciplines. Even as he entered his final decade of life Roberto Assagioli was balancing his apparently opposing activities and finding ways to make positive contributions. His beloved wife Nella's death in 1973, after a period of dementia, no doubt had a strong effect on him for the remaining year of his life. He had said that he made no decisions in life without her participation, and without his life collaborator he lived the rest of his life with a significant deficit. Assagioli had been a student of the thought of Count Hermann Keyserling since the 1920s, and had held Keyserling's writing on marriage and the couple to be significant, even saying in the 1960s that he still held *The Book of Marriage*, which was edited by Keyserling and published in 1925, to be the most important book on the subject.[14] Keyserling maintained throughout all his writing the position that the marriage relationship between a man and a woman created "a higher unity" that "corresponds exactly with an elliptical field of force." We can see that Roberto Assagioli saw the truth of this assertion and came to understand that a fully developed couple creates a new "entity" in its unity — a "couple entity."

Had he lived longer, he might have developed the ideas further, perhaps venturing into the further reaches of human experience to include aspects that had not been discussed earlier. But by the time his life was over he had lost his only son (who died of tuberculosis in 1952) and lost his wife, so clearly the "couple entity" for him personally had been irreparably shattered — although only on this plane of earthly existence, which he had explicitly indicated was, for him, only one level of many.

---

[14] Assagioli wrote an unpublished appreciation of Keyserling called "Hermann Keyserling: Master of Life" in 1971, indicating that his admiration for Keyserling remained undiminished.

Clearly more of Assagioli's thought and practice can be explored. He never taught one subject in isolation — everything was connected. And everything reaches beyond itself. We hope nevertheless that the essay that follows can provide some insight for contemporary readers and that its applicability will be not limited to the couple relationships that are present in the essay itself, but that following Assagioli, we can be both "scientific" and "poetic" in following his suggestions and teachings, to explore ever more aspects of what can constitute the psychosynthesis of the couple.

PSYCHOSYNTHESIS OF THE COUPLE
A Synthetic Essay from Portions of Writings and Talks by
ROBERTO ASSAGIOLI, MD
Presented Between 1957 and 1974
Compiled and Edited with Notes by Jan Kuniholm

This essay consists of selections from talks and lectures Dr. Assagioli gave on different occasions from 1957 to 1974.[15] This "synthetic essay" attempts to create a single narrative from portions of the talks and lectures, some of which overlap and repeat and some of which present unique material. According to Assagioli's handwritten note in Doc.#15785 of the Assagioli Archives, his sources for work on the Psychosynthesis of the Couple included works by Rabindranath Tagore, Alphonse Maeder, C.G. Jung, Beatrice Hinkle,

---

[15] Works of Roberto Assagioli, MD, and documents from Archivo Assagioli (https://www.archivioassagioli.org/) are used by permission of Istituto di Psicosintesi, Florence, Italy — http://www.psicosintesi.it/ and http://www.psicosintesi.it/english.

Richard Maurice Bucke, Alfred Adler, Lucio D'Ambra, Plato, M. Esther Harding's book The Way of All Women, *and others, especially* The Book of Marriage, *edited by Hermann Keyserling. It is apparent that Dr. Assagioli abandoned some lines of thinking that were presented in the earlier essays, and presented new perspectives in his later lectures. This essay attempts to share earlier thought that Assagioli retained while also presenting later thought that superseded his earlier positions on some things. The source materials are referenced at the end of each paragraph. At the end of this essay is a list of the sources used. Editorial elisions are shown as ". . ." and interpolations by the editor (usually done when original transcripts contain blank spaces or are unclear but suggestive) are indicated with [bracketed words]. I have standardized English language to American usage and corrected occasional incorrect English phrases without changing meaning.*

I have altered some figures of speech used in the originals that could be misconstrued by modern readers by the use of elision or bracketing; for example, where Assagioli originally used the term "man" in a way that seems as if he were making a pronouncement concerning <u>all</u> men, but which we know that he intended to mean that this quality is found <u>commonly</u> in men, I have added the bracketed word [sometimes].

Note that some of this material was previously published, but most of it was given verbally in the form of talks and lectures, and for the most part I have not attempted to "tidy up" Dr. Assagioli's spoken words for publication. Some of the transcripts were edited by Dr. Assagioli prior to their distribution to students, and some of the original unedited transcripts can be retrieved at the Assagioli Archives in Florence, Italy. Except where noted, all diagrams are those created by Roberto Assagioli in the original presentations (or reproductions of the original diagrams by this editor where they were not clear).

— Jan Kuniholm

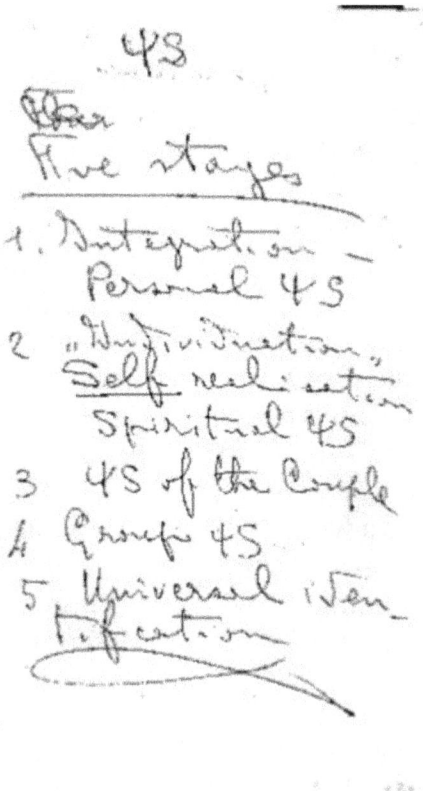

Hand-written Note by Assagioli (Archive Document #877):

ΨS (psychosynthesis):
Five stages

1. Integration - Personal psychosynthesis
2. "Individuation" - <u>Self</u> realisation -
   Spiritual ΨS (psychosynthesis)
3. ΨS (psychosynthesis) of the Couple
4. Group ΨS (psychosynthesis)
5. Universal identification

A Couple: The Smallest Psychological Group

Today, I will begin to talk about interpersonal psychosynthesis; that is, the relationships and synthesis of human couples. There are various kinds of couples, not only those made up of a husband and wife. There is the parent-child couple, teacher-student couple, and the couple between doctor and patient. There are even important couples made up of people of different sexes who are not married, such as between mother and son, father and daughter, and between collaborators of different genders. Thus, in modern society there is frequent collaboration between a manager and secretary, and in some cases also between a manager and subordinates. (1965-1 p. 1)

The field of interpersonal psychology is, therefore, very broad and encompasses a wide variety of relationships. While keeping this "framework" in mind, today we will only deal with the most common and, one might say, typical couple — the one created by the marriage relationship [between a man and a woman].[16] (1965-1 p. 1)

The theme of marriage is very difficult to deal with for various reasons. First of all, because of its great complexity and the numerous problems it presents, which concern every aspect of individual and collective human life. Secondly, it is extremely difficult to deal objectively with the theme of marriage, because it arouses in everyone a series of emotional reactions connected with positive or negative experiences that they have had or are having in this kind of relationship. (1965-1 p. 1)

Yet the subject of marriage can and must be treated scientifically, dispassionately, calmly, and impartially. In this way, and only in this way, can one see its problems in their proper light, eliminate erroneous conceptions (and there are so many!), misunderstandings, and ignorance. This is the only way to avoid so much

---

[16] At the time of Dr. Assagioli's writing, the word "marriage" was, in Europe and most contexts world-wide, reserved for a relationship between one man and one woman. —*Ed.*

unnecessary suffering and so many nerve-racking and sometimes tragic conflicts and sad failures. In this way, and only in this way, can one specify the means for harmonious and constructive solutions for the attainment of the true reasons for marriage and for the fulfillment of the great human and spiritual possibilities that it offers. (1965-1 pp. 1-2)

It is first important to clarify and recognize that many of the difficulties and conflicts often attributed to marriage and for which a spouse is held responsible are not really due to the marriage but to *human nature* itself. Marriage only reveals these conflicts, puts them into focus, so to speak, or intensifies them. Therefore, it is necessary to skillfully distinguish between the psychological problems that occur *in* marriage from those *of* marriage — that are specific to marital relations. This distinction is very useful and worthwhile on its own merit to eliminate many causes of misunderstanding and conflict, because it allows us to avoid the frequent error of blaming the spouse for difficulties and disagreements that instead are *due to ourselves*, inasmuch as we are imperfect human beings, or from circumstances and situations not attributable to either spouse. (1965-1 p. 2)

The smallest psychological group is that constituted by two individuals forming a couple. At first consideration this group might be thought to be also the simplest; yet it often raises more complicated and difficult problems than those arising in the case of much larger groups. The explanation of this paradox is that the difficulties and problems of human relations do not depend upon the size of the groups and the number of the individuals involved, but on the intensity, extension and depth of the interplay; and these are generally much greater in the case of two or a few intimately connected individuals than in the simpler and less undifferentiated actions and reactions between communities, social classes, peoples, and races. (N.D.2 p. 1)

We will first consider the most frequent [and] important kind of human couple: that constituted by a man and a woman in the constant and intimate interplay produced by the marriage relationship. Curiously enough, in spite of the vital interest which this subject has for the great majority of human beings, the psychology of the human couple is still in its infancy, and therefore the art of its synthesis is as yet embryonic, owing to the lack of necessary foundations. [17](N.D.2 p. 1)

The psychosynthesis of the couple is immensely difficult. The interplay and communion of *two* individuals does not [actually] exist. Why? Because the individual as a unified being does not exist. Instead, each person is a multiplicity of subpersonalities and has two unifying centers — the personal ego [self] and the Transpersonal Self. Therefore a couple is an interplay of relationships between multiplicities. That's a starting point. (1972 p. 1)

The communion of two individuals does not exist, because each person is a multiplicity of subpersonalities and has two unifying centers.

Complexity and Multiplicity in Every Human Being

The first and fundamental source of difficulty is the complexity and multiplicity existing in every human being. I have spoken [and written] about this several times ... but it is appropriate to stress this point because, not only is it insufficiently recognized, but even those who are convinced of it in practice, often forget it or do not take it enough into account. This complexity of our bio-psychic constitution is depicted in the diagram that I have presented several times. (1965-1 p. 2)[18]

The first distinction [in this diagram — see next page] is the three main levels of our being: the Lower, Middle and Higher Unconscious, from which continuous influences, or currents of energy,

---

[17] While much psychological work on the couple has been done since Assagioli's time, the art of synthesis with respect to couples has not necessarily been part of the work. —*Ed.*

[18] Assagioli used this "egg diagram" in both of his published books and uses variations of it later in this essay, in his analysis of the kinds of relationships that men and women engage in. —*Ed.*

Psychosynthesis of the Couple

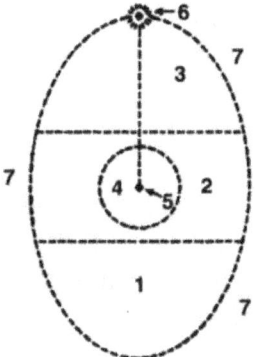

Diagram 1
1. The Lower Unconscious
2. The Middle Unconscious
3. The Higher Unconscious or Superconscious
4. The Field of Consciousness
5. The Conscious Self or "I"
6. The Higher Self
7. The Collective Unconscious

flow into the field of consciousness, which can be considered as the battlefield between all these influences that are diverse in nature, origin, and value. At the center of consciousness is the conscious "I" [personal self], which is generally flooded by these contents and gradually identifies itself with one and the other. Therefore, this center of consciousness has no stability, coherence, or peace. In the best cases, the influences of the spiritual [Transpersonal or Higher] Self also reach the "I," which, on the one hand is a help, but on the other, is also a complication, in that the influx of spiritual energies creates new problems and conflicts. (1965-1 pp. 2-3)

The influx of spiritual energies creates new problems and conflicts.

We can draw important practical deductions from this. The first is that we must, above all, work to realize our own psychosynthesis; or, more realistically, to gain a certain measure of control and regulation over our contrasting tendencies and internal "characters" [or subpersonalities]. Obviously, if there are conflicts or conflicting subpersonalities within us, we cannot be in harmony with another person. In fact, our subpersonality "A" may be in harmony with our spouse, while our subpersonality "B" is in conflict. And the same can be happening for the other partner. (1965-1 p. 3)

The second deduction is that since the other, the spouse, has the same difficulties and the same problems as we do, we must not blame him or her, but tolerate the situation and accept the consequences. We often tend to expect that others (and not just our spouse!) to be better than we actually are ourselves, and this is not fair. Instead each one of us should help each other to achieve his or her own psychosynthesis — and not only out of affection, but also for our own benefit through mutual understanding. (1965-1 p. 3)

The spouse has the same problems as we do.

Differential Psychology of Men and Women

The first basis required [for considering the psychology of the couple] is a satisfactory differential psychology of man and woman, and while countless observations, remarks and opinions have been expressed on this matter throughout the ages, they are often unreliable and contradict each other; and in many cases they clearly appear to be outbursts of individual personal experience rather than even an attempt at a considered and objective appraisal. . . . Only in comparatively recent times have serious attempts been made to build up a scientific differential psychology of the sexes; and a certain amount of reliable facts have been collected. (N.D.2 p. 1)

But the task is far from being completed. Even if it were, it would not be at all sufficient. Each of the individuals forming the couple, besides being a man or woman in general, belongs to a definite psychological type; and if we take into consideration the seven types of the qualitative classification, we see how many are the possible combinations, each of which should

Each person in a couple belongs to one of seven psychological types, and functions in four different field or levels of life. We should consider the interplay of individuals on each of these levels.

be separately studied.[19] Then there is, as we have seen in dealing with the fundamental types, the fact that each human being functions in four different fields or levels of life, although in varying proportions: the physical, the emotional, the mental, and the intuitive [see diagram on page 29]. Therefore, in studying any couple we should consider the interplay of the individuals in question on each of those levels. (N.D.2 p. 1)

In most marriages, the union is based only on physical, emotional or social factors, and we note that after some time of intoxication, a "substantial" union — something that should last — hardly exists. [The partners] do not know enough what a great adventure marriage is; what an effort of adaptation it requires; and what physical, emotional, mental and even spiritual conflicts it causes. In many cases, the spouses know each other too little and unite instantly with a sudden and unreasoning impulse. They do not count on the time that is required to reveal certain aspects [of their relationship] that are sometimes very unexpected. The common life of two beings who coexist intimately ... each bringing their own habits, tastes, and comforts, sometimes causes friction due to the lack of understanding and detachment. We easily understand then, that if there is no more fundamental bond than physical or emotional attraction between them, conflicts are not long in coming — especially if in addition, practical issues such as money and health present difficulties. It is therefore obvious that unions which are based on more solid

In most marriages, after some time of intoxication, a "substantial" union hardly exists.

Time is required to reveal certain aspects of a relationship, that may be very unexpected.

---

[19] The seven human types are, according to Assagioli, The Will Type, The Love Type, The Active-Practical Type, The Creative-Artistic Type, The Scientific Type, The Devotional-Idealistic Type, and The Organizational Type. For more information about the seven types, see *Psychosynthesis Typology,* by Roberto Assagioli, MD, published in 2004 by the Institute of Psychosynthesis, London. https://www.psychosynthesis.org/. A more recent treatment has been made by Kenneth Sørensen in his book *The Seven Types: Psychosynthesis Typology - Discover Your Five Dominant Types* (2019).

Psychosynthesis of the Couple

foundations than the above-mentioned are more likely to succeed and prosper, as they are based on a more genuine and deep attraction. It is easier for two beings who are [already] united on the soul level to apply themselves, little by little, to harmonize their two personalities, than for them to start from an [emotional or physical] attraction on the personal level and attempt to successfully create a soul connection. (N.D.1 pp. 2-3)

The psychological constitutions of man and woman are more different than we generally realize.

The psychological constitutions of man and woman are deeply different, much more so than we generally realize. It therefore seems useful to pause and examine somewhat the differing characteristics of male and female psychology. (1968 p. 2)

Let us [look again at] the fundamental polarities of man and woman. There is a fundamental typological difference between man and woman ... [which is] the cause of constant misunderstandings and conflicts. They are not sufficiently known or recognized; first of all, because of psychological ignorance. There are all possible differentiations and differences, type percentages and so on. I have illustrated this in a diagram - a **"Scheme of Man's and Woman's Bio-Psychical Characteristics."** [20] (1958 p. 1 and 1965-1 p. 3)

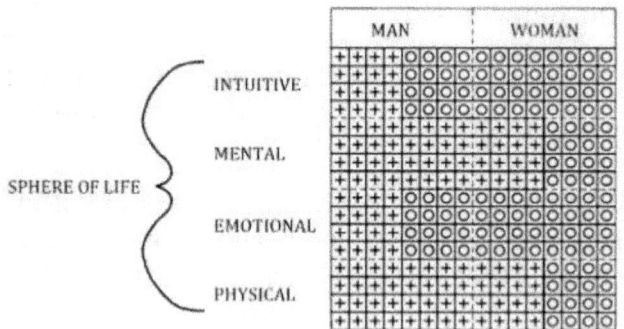

---

[20] This diagram clearly represents *average tendencies* in thought, emotion, and behavior, etc. in men and women. Research since his time has supported this assessment. Assagioli speaks of one sex or the other being more or less developed in each area, but see also his developed thought concerning masculine and feminine principles on pages 71-73 of this essay, which were also considered by this writer on pages 15-17. —*Ed.*

We can say that between woman and man there exists an "inverted" polarity. (1965-1 p. 3) Typically, although by no means universally, there exists between a husband and his wife polarities of psychological functions. The man tends to excel in certain vital operations while the woman manifests others. (1968 p. 2) In the average, normal man of the active, sensation type (1958 p. 1), man has active, dynamic, constructive functions... In the emotional and imaginative sphere, the polarity is different: here [the average] woman is more positive, active and better developed, while man is apt to be more easily influenced.[21] In the intellectual field we have another inversion of the polarity: here man is eminently active .. while woman in this domain is [on average] less developed and active. [22] But there is another sphere often disregarded, that of the intuition, in which woman is often developed and man is not. (1965-1 pp. 3-4) So there is an apparent inversion of dominant functions that man and woman need to appreciate, and therefore collaborate with each other in order to form an effective team. (1968 p. 3)

Typically there is an "inverted polarity" between woman and man: they need to appreciate the differences in their dominant functions and collaborate with each other to form an effective team.

I have purposely exaggerated my description of extreme cases in order to drive home my point with greater efficacy and to make clear what I want to establish. Fortunately, in reality, things are better than that, or ... at least, not so bad! (1965-1 p. 5)

---

[21] Assagioli's use of the word "type" in this sentence refers to one of the "seven human types" developed in the psychosynthesis typology. See note 19 above. —*Ed.*

[22] Note here the use of the word "intellectual," as opposed to "mental," which Dr. Assagioli has used elsewhere. "Intellectual" pursuits often involve the skill of abstraction, at which a male often excels. "Mental" efforts, on the other hand, may also involve the skill of integration, at which a female often excels. It appears that in his discussion of the differences between men and women, Assagioli often means "intellectual" in the sense we use here, and not the wider term "mental" in the wider sense. This may be a matter of the nuances of language moving from Italian to English.—*Ed.*

[This typological difference is something] we have to keep well in mind for the psychosynthesis of the couple. In reality, matters are not simple, because [of] all the reactions and other compensations ... so, this balance between man and woman is the most intimate and personal problem and one of the widest social problems at the same time. (1958 pp. 1-2)

To these different polarities correspond important qualitative distinctions, which can explain many deficiencies, derangements and nervous and psychological troubles. These differences have been keenly and deeply studied by Jung, who has been a pioneer in this obscure and complicated field. (1965-1 p. 4)

It is easy to see how ... one-sided development and the deficiencies they engender can cause serious injury. For men and women are in themselves incomplete psychologically, almost maimed beings. They can find the solution of their problems only through mutual integration, by combining their qualities so as to constitute together, a psychologically complete human being. (1965-1 p. 5)

There are some prerequisites in the psychosynthesis of the couple and the first is, I think, the acceptance of their respective roles, and the mutual respect and appreciation of those respective roles, which go hand in hand — easily said, but very difficult to accomplish; but it is a pre-requisite for the psychosynthesis of the couple. [23] Here, in this [set of] diagrams [on the next page], I have indicated the possible situations in the man-woman relationship.[24]

---

[23] It will be seen later in this essay that Dr. Assagioli did not retain a conviction in *fixed* or unchanging roles associated with either men or women; so it may be inferred here that the respective "roles" of men and women are those that arise naturally or evolve out of the unique character of a particular relationship. Recognition, decision, respect and appreciation naturally precede acceptance. —Ed.

[24] These are based upon the "egg diagram," which lists the meaning of the three levels, presented earlier (page 26). — Ed.

Psychosynthesis of the Couple

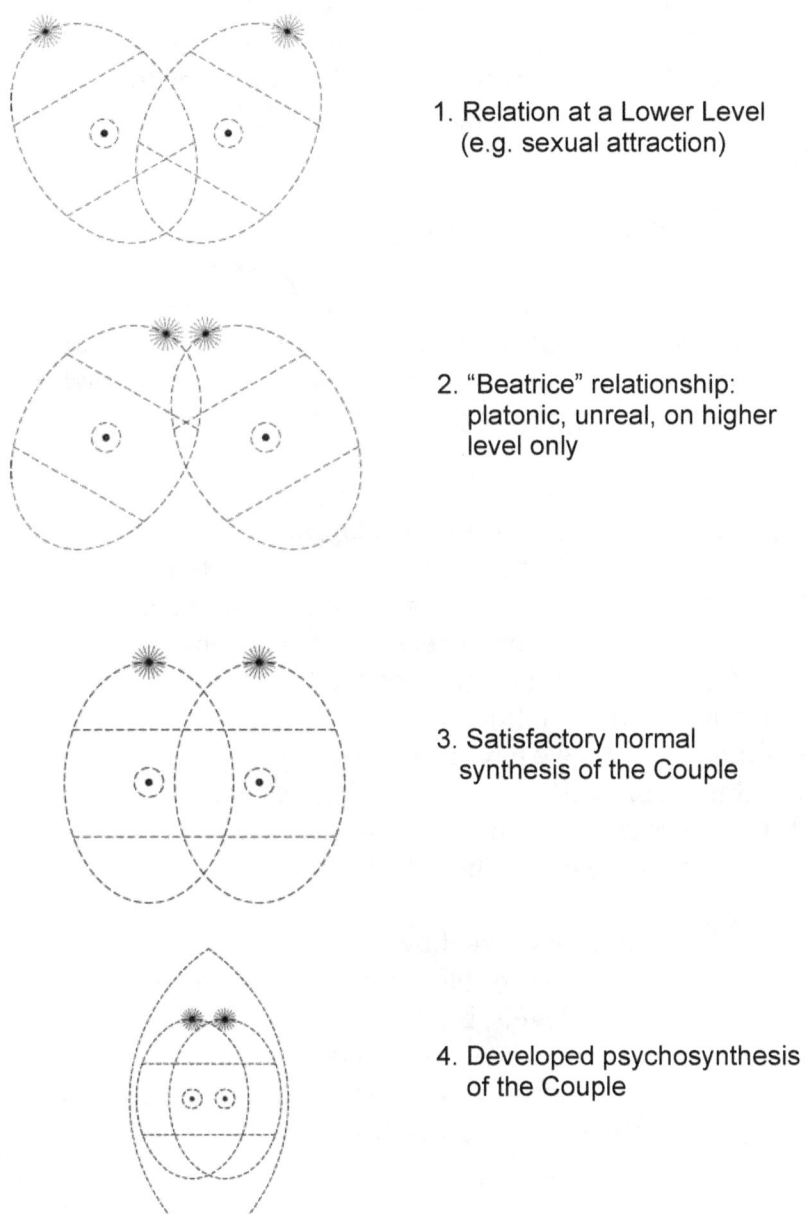

1. Relation at a Lower Level (e.g. sexual attraction)

2. "Beatrice" relationship: platonic, unreal, on higher level only

3. Satisfactory normal synthesis of the Couple

4. Developed psychosynthesis of the Couple

1) Here [in diagram #1], we have the unfortunately frequent situation in which there is very partial synthesis — it does

32

not really deserve the name of synthesis, but is really relationship and passion blending on the lower level. That is a typical case of purely sexual attraction which attracts the lower part of both with no participation of the self, just the physical relationships, fleeting or more or less lasting.

The second diagram shows the opposite. It could be called "platonic" love, in which there is a relationship on the higher level, but it is a false relationship, with suppression of the other relationships on other levels and with no real human participation, only a mutual aspiring to the higher which cannot last because it is only natural (in the good sense of the word).

2) Here, we have [in] the [third, a] diagram of the satisfactory normal synthesis of the couple — not complete, but fairly advanced. Here there is the participation of each self partially in the life of the other. There is an amount of physical blending, a great amount of emotional and mental blending, a certain amount of higher — let us call it spiritual — blending.[25] So here we have a good example of psychosynthesis of the couple with partial blending; each is not lost in the other, each retains his and her individuality but participates consciously in the life of the other.

And in [diagram] #4, we have a much more developed psychosynthesis of the couple, harmonious on all levels, more or less equal on all levels, but it goes *beyond* the couple. The relationships are the same as in the [third] diagram, but here the prolongation goes below — below in the good sense — and above with a common public task [such as] in the

---

[25] Even though this essay was originally presented by Dr. Assagioli in English, it is reasonable to question the use of the word "blending" in this section. In modern usage we distinguish "blending" which creates a homogeneous "soup" over against a "stew," a kind of intimate union in which the identity of ingredients is retained. While there may truly be some "blending" in relationships illustrated in Diagrams #1 and #2, the intimate union is the more likely product in those illustrated in Diagrams #3 and #4.—*Ed.*

education of children. In the life of the couple there is a *common* life in the world, and beyond the personal relationship there is a common spiritual life activity which can be religious, humanitarian or that kind. So that is *beyond* the couple; the couple is not lost in itself, but is in contact with other human beings and all their activities. This marks a step from the first psychosynthesis of the couple to the synthesis of groups. (1958 pp. 2-3)

Stages of Union

We can very schematically represent the different stages of the union of two beings by the following drawings:

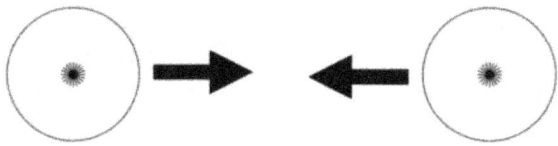

Drawing #1

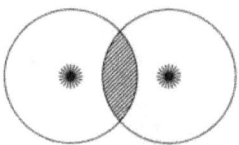

Drawing #2

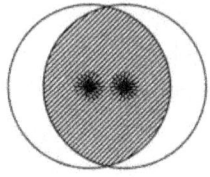

Drawing #3

Psychosynthesis of the Couple

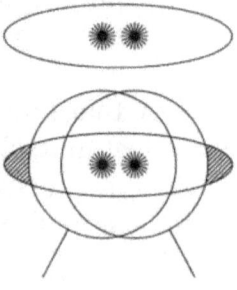

Drawing #4

In Drawing #1, the circles represent the personalities of the two individuals, and the center points are their centers of consciousness. There is an attraction in the majority of cases based upon emotional and physical affinities. In #2, the two individuals have pooled part of their personalities, that is to say that in certain parts of their emotional and mental body, there are points which have been pooled by the two individuals through deeper mutual knowledge. But this union does not yet include the centers of consciousness which remain independent.

It is only after very deep contact and a large number of common experiences (drawing #3) that the centers of consciousness are on a common ground for the two individuals. Even in marriage, this state is rarely reached. There is then a fundamental understanding of the two beings on the three personality planes: physical, emotional, mental. It is at this moment that the strength of the couple is greatest, because two individual energies are then pooled for the benefit of a new entity. The couple is not only responsible for the unification of the conscious energies of each individual, but also of their unconscious forces, which then seem not only to function on the level of the individual personality, but also on that of the new personality, which becomes "the couple." Two spouses who have achieved such a union have a great coherence in executing plans of action, which does not exclude their personal independence.

This new entity is represented in [the upper portion of] drawing #4 by an ellipse: the ellipse indeed has the remarkable property of depending on two focal points while the circle — which is only a special case of the ellipse — has only one. Likewise the couple depends on the two centers of consciousness; it exceeds the limits of a single personality. The darkened part of the ellipse [in the lower portion of drawing #4], which exceeds the two circles, represents the creations of the couple: on the physical level this is expressed by children; on the emotional level, by the love and the devotion of the spouses one for the other and for the children. On the mental level, there can be cooperation in various activities, in particular the education of children. We therefore see that the most important work of the spouses is to achieve the most nearly total union on all levels in order to be able to use the maximum energy to achieve common goals. This union is only possible if each strives to forget individual desires in favor of the requirements of the couple. (N.D.1 pp. 3-4)

The couple depends on two centers of consciousness; it exceeds the limits of a single personality.

Several things must be considered with regard to the notion of balance in the couple. First, the authority must be divided equally, each of the spouses having fifty percent of both responsibility and initiative; for if one of the spouses has a lesser share [in this balance], the relations one will have with the other will no longer be those which characterize spouses but rather children, or even slaves. The will to control is inherent in [many men]. It is normal for [such a man] to look after [a woman]; but he must know how [to] maintain a balance. In marriage, each must place a certain amount of their will to control — half of the authority — in the couple. As for the rest, which should not be repressed, a man will use it either in

In marriage, each partner must place a certain amount of their will to control - half of the authority - in the couple.

Psychosynthesis of the Couple

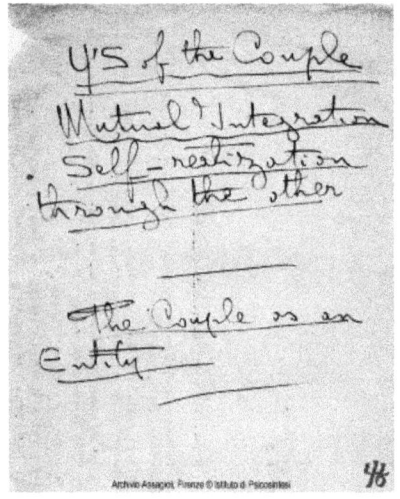

Hand-written Note by Assagioli
(Archive Document #15763):

ΨS (Psychosynthesis)
of the Couple
Mutual integration
Self-realization
through the other

—

The Couple as an Entity

—

his work, in sport, or in self-control. Women can use theirs in the education of children and in [their other activities]. It is absolutely necessary to avoid the states of "matriarchy" or "patriarchy" which are too often the occasion of a very unhappy despotism. [When such unbalanced states prevail in a relationship], indeed, how could a child have a true image of the father in a "matriarchy" where the mother makes all the decisions and takes on the specific functions of a man? Likewise, in many couples, the woman is reduced to the state of tacit servant and subjected [to] the authority of an angry tyrannical husband. (N.D.1 pp. 4-5)

[Men and women] have specific functions which they must fulfill to maintain the balance of the couple, and especially to serve as an example for the children. Because it should not be forgotten that when the children become parents in their turn, they will instinctively take the same attitudes as those of their parents. If this image was distorted, either they will react by an opposite excess; or more simply, their conduct will be affected by their parents' shortcomings. (N.D.1 p. 5)

Then there is a deeper and more obscure problem. According to Jung's acute analysis, each man harbors in his unconscious a feminine psychological aspect, which constitutes an inner image which [Jung] calls "anima;" and each woman has in her unconscious a masculine image, the "animus." Jung's conception is certainly open to discussion; but we may consider unquestionable that in each man there is a more or less developed and a more or less unconscious feminine side, and vice versa. This psychological bisexuality — which is perfectly normal, and should in no way be confused with sexual inversion — arouses different reactions and has different effects in the various individuals. [26] (N.D.2 pp. 1-2)

> Each man has a feminine aspect in his unconscious and each woman has a masculine aspect in her unconscious.

One of the most frequent reactions is the attempt [by people] to deny and suppress the complementary part in themselves. This is done chiefly by men, through a mistaken and one-sided ideal of "one-hundred-percent masculinity." Thus they feel ashamed of their emotional or imaginative life and carefully inhibit all expression of it.... Other men cherish the idea of the aggressive "go-getter," and forcefully suppress the tempering grace of conscious feeling and real humanity.... Another variety of the same attitude is that of men who, having by constitution a well-developed emotional nature which is present in them, react to it by overcompensation and develop a rigidly objective [attitude] and relentless, often cruel behavior.[27] ... All such reactions prevent the harmonious development of the individual and his psychosynthesis, but are apt to produce serious troubles of a collective kind, such as those which are now happening [in the world] under our eyes. [28] (N.D.2 p. 2)

---

[26] The word bisexuality is used in reference to Jung's concepts only, and does not refer to the modern sense of "sexual orientation." —*Ed*

[27] Such reactions and the attitudes that arise from them are seldom conscious decisions on the part of individuals, but more often are created and reinforced by cultural norms which vary widely from group to group, nation to nation, area to area. Assagioli's original essay, following Keyserling, associated certain attitudes with specific European nations, in which such attitudes seemed common in the early decades of the 20th century. It comes as a surprise to many people when they discover that their attitudes are often not a result of their own choices, but are rather a determinant of those choices in many cases.—*Ed.*

[28] The manuscript was not dated; most probably "now" is the 1930s or 1950s.—*Ed.*

A second reaction, even more mistaken, is that of devaluing and trying to suppress the psychological qualities of one's own sex and trying to develop and express chiefly those of the opposite one. This reaction has been often demonstrated in recent times by [some] women, particularly through certain excesses of the feminist movement.[29] It is right to recognize that the original incentive and urge of modern women to react against both the excessive development of their "feminine" traits and functions to the exclusion of the complementary and compensating ones, and also against the outer [social] limitations and conditions of inferiority, was right and necessary. Much benefit derived to women, to society, and to men themselves from the change of a "mere woman" into a well-developed and integrated human being. (N.D.2 p. 2)

> *Denial of the complementary part in ourselves prevents the harmonious development of the individual and produces serious collective troubles.*

But there are other . . . constructive issues. In the individual's conscious or unconscious urge towards integration three solutions, or attempts towards solution, are possible:

> The first is *independent self-integration*, attempted through the [individual] development of [one's own] complementary aspect (the feminine in the case of a man, and [the masculine in women]), and its integration with the fundamental one.[30]

---

[29] The essay from which this paragraph was extracted was presented in the 1950s or 1960s, when feminists' novel self-assertive behavior was shocking to many in the older generations, some of whom regarded such behavior as "masculine." In more recent times many behaviors have been liberated from gender stereotypes. Assagioli clearly believed in fundamental equality (but not the "sameness") of the sexes, but at this time he seems to be writing from the norms that prevailed throughout the first three-quarters of his life. He was quoted in the early 1970s as saying that he had "outgrown the *zeitgeist*" [spirit of the time] of his youth. —*Ed.*

[30] It seems important to stress here that the integration Assagioli is referring to here is *individual* integration, not the integration of the couple. In the first example, the integration is done alone, which is why Assagioli says below that in this case the person remains *psychologically* single, whether technically "married" or not. —*Ed.*

The second is *indirect self-integration*, achieved through the help of a person of the other sex, whose influence helps to awaken, make conscious and develop the complementary aspect [within the person].

The third is *external integration*. In this case the integration is sought and achieved *outside* of the individual. The man remains outstandingly masculine, and experiences the complementary aspect only through the woman who lives at his side; and vice versa.

In the first case the individual remains psychologically single, whether he [or she] is married or not; in the second and third cases the couple as a psychological entity comes into existence, but functions in different ways. The psychological interactions which take place within the couple and between the two elements which have composed it are manifold and intricate. They involve the investigation of the laws of psychological polarity, an investigation which in great part has yet to be made. It involves also the study of the principle and of the laws of "triangularity;" that is, of the synthesis of two polar elements achieved, not through the mere interaction between themselves, but by the intervention and the action of a third element. A few instances will make clear some of the concrete situations and possibilities. In the polar relationship expressing itself exclusively, or almost so, in the physical and emotional realms, as in the case of passionate or romantic love, there is a natural absorption of the two individuals, with a marked isolation from other influences and interchanges, manifesting as an *égoisme à deux* [selfishness for two]. This may be a more or less temporary stage, which is followed by that of a triangular interplay, in which

> The "laws of triangularity" come into play when the integration of two elements is achieved by the intervention and action of a third element.

the third element may be constituted either by a child and the interest and affection it evokes, or in a common purpose, in a common task, in a common spiritual ideal. In some cases the triple interplay exists from the beginning of the relationship. (N.D.2 pp. 2-3)

[Another] difficulty is due to typological differences that are independent of gender. I mentioned the four fundamental types, corresponding to the four functions: sensation, feeling, thought, and intuition. In addition, there are also the *extroverts* and *introverts*. It was to Jung's merit that he highlighted this important difference with regard to the direction of one's vital interests — either towards the external world or towards the internal world. (1965-1 p. 7)

This distinction, however, must be more fully explained and refined. Both introversion and extroversion can be active or passive. There is a great difference between active and passive extroverts. Active extroverts are typically men of action; by contrast, passive extroversion consists of a special power of attraction which influences objects and persons and a particular receptivity to their influence. Passive extroverts are sensitive, impressionable, and dependent on external circumstances, for example, a person who "agrees with the last one who spoke." A typical expression of passive extroversion is reading the newspaper. (1965-1 p. 7)

In addition to their typological differences, people may be introverted or extroverted — sometimes introverted on one level and extroverted on another — and this presents another challenge to couples' mutual understanding.

No less important are the differences between active introverts and passive introverts. In passive introversion there is a lack of interest in the external world due to self-centeredness and concern for oneself. Active introversion, on the other hand, is a conscious, voluntary detachment from the external world to carry out a positive action in the internal world. A typical example of this is an interest in psychology and activities in this field. (1965-1 p. 7)

But there is a further differentiation and complication: one can be extroverted at one level and introverted at another. For example, one can be extroverted in the level of sensitivity, and introverted in the world of thought; so there is a wide range of combinations, upon which I cannot dwell now. (1965-1 p. 7)

All these factors create difficulties in mutual understanding. Sensory and emotional types do not understand mental types. Mental types do not understand intuitive types, and vice-versa. In turn, extroverts and introverts do not understand each other — but above all, extroverts [usually] do not understand or appreciate introverts. These great individual differences constitute obstacles to mutual understanding and, therefore, to mutual agreement in general, but especially in the continuous and intimate life of a family. (1965-1 p. 7)

Fortunately, however, it is almost always a question of the *prevalence* of certain characteristics, not of their exclusive presence or absence. Therefore, there is always a more or less large — or small — common ground or area of similarity or affinity to use as a basis from which to begin mutual understanding and psychosynthesis. (1965-1 p. 7)

There is always a common ground or area of similarity to use as a basis to begin mutual understanding and psychosynthesis.

The same is true of the active or passive disposition. The most dynamic man, the most active woman, when they are at the cinema or watching television, become *passive* extroverts for that hour or two. Given this, everyone should strive to alternate harmoniously and appropriately between the opposing tendencies, moderating the excessive manifestations of those of his or her own psychological type. (1965-1 p. 9)

But there is another important fact which is often ignored or not taken into due consideration: no human being exists and manifests itself *only* in its [own] nature and in its masculine or feminine functions. In every human being there is a part — always greater the more the person has evolved — which is *outside* and *above* those specific functions. Therefore, every human being must be considered and treated *first and foremost* as a "person," with his or her dignity, value, and purpose as such. Women who have this awareness and affirm it feel offended and angry, and rightly so, when they are considered only, or above all else, as female, as an object of sexual satisfaction. Even at a higher level, there are men who see in every woman *only*, or almost only, someone who has the function of wife, or mother of his children. But also, inversely, there are women who see in their male partners, *only* a husband, a father of her children with the duties that come with these roles. (1965-1 pp. 7-8)

No person exists and manifests only in its own nature and in masculine or feminine functions. There is always a part outside and above those functions. Every human being is first and foremost a "person."

As important and noble as these functions are, they do not constitute and must not absorb the *whole* human being. In each person there are aspects, feelings, and activities *other than* those functions: there are mental activities, the search for truth, a moral sense, aesthetic sense, social sense, altruistic love, and religious feelings that are independent of gender. All these can be "colored" [i.e. shaded or influenced or given a different look] by one's gender and they can be areas and occasions in which one's gender manifests itself, but they are *essentially* independent of gender. (1965-1 p. 8)

Higher Perspectives

But there is more. The spiritual Self, the highest and truest part of us, is free from any polarity that could be called "horizontal."

Its polarization is "vertical;" that is, with the conscious "I" that is a projection or reflection of the Higher Self. And the more the "I", the center of the human personality, approaches the Self, the more it "recognizes" itself in it, to the point of identifying with the Self, and the more the human being is then free from the determinations and characteristics of his or her sex, as well as those of his or her own psychological type. (1965-1 p. 8)

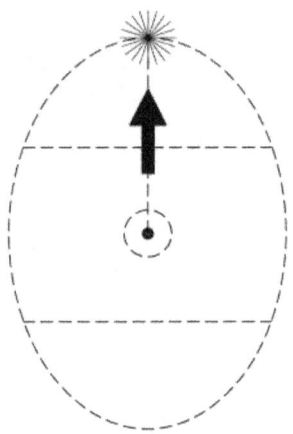

"I" Moves toward Identification with Self
[*Diagram by Editor*]

What is desirable is the manifestation of the *higher* characteristics, the better qualities of the other sex. Among men, often poets, artists, and musicians have had and expressed the feminine qualities of sensitivity, subtle feelings, and intuitions. An eminent example, among many, was [Italian poet] Giovanni Pascoli . . . [and] among women there are illustrious examples . . . [such as] Joan of Arc, . . . Florence Nightingale . . . [and] the Countess Gabriella Spalletti Rasponi, who promoted the foundation of [the Psychosynthesis] Institute in Rome in 1926. . . The reciprocal qualities of the sexes, *in their higher aspects*, are a useful, indeed necessary, common ground of mutual understanding and cooperation, and make the couple's psychosynthesis possible. (1965-1 p. 6)

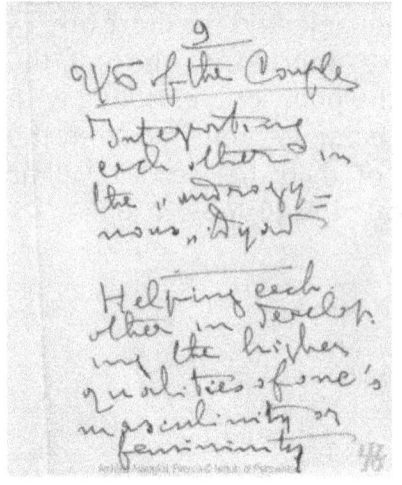

Hand-written Note by Assagioli –
Archive Document #15607

ΨS (Psychosynthesis)
of the Couple
Integrating each other
in the "androgynous" Dyad

—

Helping each other in
developing the higher qualities
of one's masculinity or femininity

Furthermore, one can confirm a fact, which at first may seem paradoxical to state, that the more a person is released from (not identified with) those psycho-sexual definitions, the better he or she can perform the specific activities of his or her own sex and avoid its limitations and exaggerations. A mother who has her own personal life with cultural, religious, and social interests, is a *better mother* than one who is exclusively "maternal." She can dedicate less actual time to her children; but the time that she gives them has a value and dignity, and produces an educational effect that is much greater than the time given by the woman who is exclusively "maternal," who is often possessive and jealous. This is an important point. There is no opposition or conflict between the parts of the personality that are independent of the psychosexual constitution and the necessary typical activities that everyone performs as a man or woman.
(1965-1 p. 8)

All this concerns the broad category of what I have called psychological problems *in marriage*. But I repeat that they are not specific to marriage; they exist in all interpersonal relationships. They should be known, addressed and at least to some extent, preferably resolved *before* marriage through appropriate education and preparation of young people; but, if not, then, at least *during* marriage. In this way, and only in this way, can young people avoid the criticisms, reproaches, and accusations that poison so many marriages; and instead, the spouses can help each other to eliminate the causes of conflicts and to form *the psychosynthesis of the couple.* (1965-1 p. 8)

... We need to examine its highest and most essential aspect, that of the spiritual communion between the spouses and their united and concordant participation with the supra-individual spiritual Reality. In psychological terms they can be called:

1. The communion between the spiritual Self of the two spouses.
2. The recognition — the lived experience — of the union, of the *identity* of the individual selves with the universal Self.

This neutral language adapts to any metaphysical or religious conception that one may have. On the other hand, the recognition in this scientific, psychological sense, of the reality of the spiritual Self and its intimate relationships with other selves and with the Supreme Reality opens the door, so to speak, to all superconscious experience of every belief or faith. (1965-2 p. 1)

The methods to arrive at this spiritual communion are the same as those used to achieve individual psychosynthesis. On this occasion I can only list them: they are meditation, prayer, invocation, "inner listening," followed by inspiration and illumination. With their use, the personal "I" increasingly recognizes its essential identity with the spiritual Self, "rises," and approaches it, until it realizes a more or less temporary and complete identification. (1965-2 p. 1)

> *The methods for spiritual communion are the same as for individual psychosynthesis: meditation, prayer, "inner listening," followed by inspiration and illumination.*

When these methods are used together by a couple, by the two spouses, a doubly beneficial result is obtained. Because of their reciprocal influences, the exchanges at every level that occur naturally and inevitably in every interpersonal relationship, and also because of the "cross biopsychological polarity,"... meditating, praying, and "inner listening" become much more effective. Furthermore, in mutually communicating what has been perceived in receptive silence there is often a mutual integration, and also the possibility of regulation and mutual correction. For example, one of the spouses (most often the woman) can "grasp" a symbolic image, and the other help to interpret and understand it. (1965-2 p. 1)

> *Because of reciprocal influences, meditating, praying and "inner listening" become much more effective when used together by a couple.*

Furthermore, this common shared "inner activity" facilitates and increases the spiritual communion between the partners, and their integration and synthesis at every level. In fact, these methods can and should also be used to solve problems and eliminate the conflicts of cohabitation. Dealing with human problems in the light of the Spirit, asking for light and guidance from the superconscious and from the spiritual Self, depersonalizes, so to speak, these problems and eliminates or attenuates the emotional reactions that activate and complicate them. This greatly facilitates their solution, and can sometimes be the only way to reach a solution and to attain a real and solid psychosynthesis of the couple. (1965-2 p. 1)

In reality, "assigning labels," making classifications, has only a relative importance. Instead it is very important to *distinguish the lower aspects and the higher aspects* of any human characteristic and to *use the means and techniques to transmute the lower into higher aspects.* (1965-1 p. 9)

Mutual Respect and Ideal Images

Respect for the personality of the other and recognition of his or her right *to be him or herself* are essential, not only for a true and proper psychosynthesis of the couple, but also for avoiding the quarrels and conflicts that embitter married life and endanger its continuity. That respect and recognition require, above all, the understanding that *perfect* fusion and consonance (which are the ideal and pretense of "romantic love") are unachievable — and are not even to be hoped for, because they would produce an "egotistical twosome." They also require the relinquishment of two strong tendencies that are inherent in human nature: that of wanting to shape the spouse in one's own image and likeness, and that of wanting to shape the other according to *one's own idea* or "ideal image" of a person of the opposite sex. (1965-3 p. 4)

Perfect fusion and consonance between partners are unachievable and not even to be hoped for, because they would produce an "egotistical twosome."

A serious complication in the achievement of a satisfactory psychosynthesis of the couple — something that has been pointed out and described by psychoanalysts — is that of the subconscious image or ideal of the opposite sex, which a man or a woman has developed. Its origin is generally to be found in the positive or negative impression made on the child and the adolescent by [the] parent of the opposite sex. Such an image is later [often] projected by young men or women upon the person they love, or believe they love. This creates in the couple a double illusion and a consequent series of misunderstandings which is one of the most frequent causes of unhappiness. Therefore a clear-sighted analysis of one's subconscious in this respect, as well as in others, is a necessary condition for the successful achievement of the delicate task of the couple's psychosynthesis, and we hope it will be recognized as a duty [to oneself and to one's partner] in [a future] era more conscious of psychological realities. (N.D.2 p. 3)

A subconscious image or ideal of the opposite sex can be a serious complication for the psychosynthesis of the couple.

Another important point to be taken into constant consideration is that both men and women have lower and higher psychological characteristics which should be well known and discriminated, and that in the attempt to reach any of the above-mentioned psychosynthesis solutions the constant endeavor should be to develop and elicit (demonstrate) the higher qualities of the opposite sex, and not his or her faults, although it is easier to demonstrate the latter than the former! (N.D.2 p. 3)

[Let us now revisit some material from a slightly different angle, with the following diagrams.]

Various Types and Degrees of Psychosynthesis

I. Extent or Amount of Communication

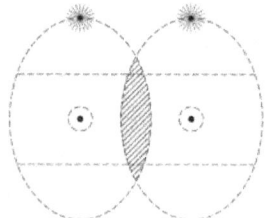
A. Little Communication

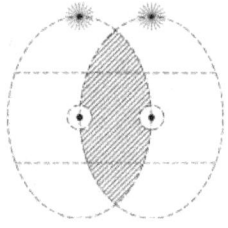
B. Greater Amount

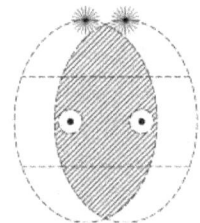
C. Higher

II. Levels of Communication

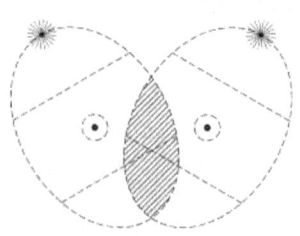
A. Chiefly on Lower Levels

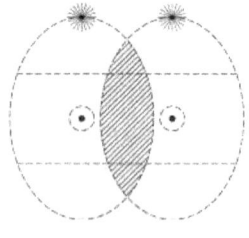
B. All Levels the Same

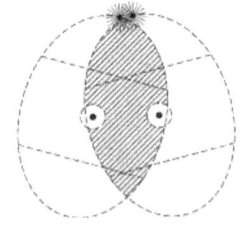
C. Chiefly on Higher Levels

A is mostly physical and/or emotional;
B has about the same communication on all three levels;
C is chiefly at the higher levels. This is the level of *communion*. [31]

Differences in Intensity

1. Communication   2. Interplay   3. Communion

Each requires the previous one but not the higher; there can be communication with little interplay and no communion. Communion in its highest stages reaches to identification. (1972 p. 1)

With regard to all the diagrams, it must be remembered that the situations represented by them are not static or permanent. Changes of various kinds can happen — indeed, they always do happen: changes of moving closer or distancing oneself; that is, attraction and contact or detachment and even repulsion. Furthermore, variations and developments can occur in relationships which could be indicated by changes in the inclination [or tilt] of the egg diagrams that represent the two people. A frequent case is that of a relationship beginning with a prevailing sexual attraction [such as in Diagram II-A], which then develops in affectivity and also in mental understanding. Sometimes the beginning is purely emotional, sentimental and passionate with subsequent mutual understanding, in the best cases, on both the physical and spiritual levels. At other times the beginning is "at the highest level" [as in Diagram II-C]. It is a spiritual understanding, with subsequent integration of the other levels. (1965-3 pp. 4-5)

---

[31] It is important for us to keep in mind that Assagioli was aware that diagrams are necessarily simplifications, meant to augment verbal discussion and practice but not to replace them. Nevertheless, certain subtleties are evident in the way his diagrams present interactions: for example, notice that "I" and the conscious "field of awareness" (labeled #4 and #5 in the original "egg diagram" presented on page 26) of each person increasingly interact as one moves from Diagram I-A to I-C. A similar change occurs in Diagrams II-A, B, and C.
One commentator has questioned the use of these diagrams to depict interaction between people, but it seems appropriate that Assagioli is trying to depict the individual impacts of interaction, and the diagrams show how much of these interactions are in fact unconscious. —*Ed.*

Reason for Difficulties

At present, difficulties are increased by the rapid changes going on [in people]. But let us make the best of this situation. I am speaking for those who are willing to work at the task of psychosynthesis in the marriage. Sometimes both partners are willing to cooperate; sometimes only one is willing, but if only one is willing it is still possible to achieve the psychosynthesis to some degree. (1972 p. 1)

Elimination of Obstacles

1. One great obstacle is due to *projection*. There is a natural tendency to project the "images" that are in us onto the partner. The man [sometimes] projects on his wife the feminine image of his mother or of other women from early life, or the ideal image of what he thinks women should be. The woman [sometimes] projects her image of her father upon her husband. She is [sometimes] looking for a "father" or her ideal image... Both [might be] doing the same thing — a "Comedy of Errors."[32] To be aware of *projections* clears the ground and is a constant process. (1972 p. 2)

2. Next, and more genuine in a sense, is the *drive to dominate*.[33] It is based on self-assertion and self-centeredness and often results in aggressive behavior. There is a close relationship between self-assertion and sex. Sex is [sometimes] used as a means of self-assertion as the man tries to conquer the woman and the woman attracts the man to dominate him. There is a constant interplay between

---

[32] A reference to Shakespeare's famous play in which two sets of identical twins, thought to be lost to each other, are in the same city unbeknownst to each other, and are switched so that the wife of one thinks she is with the other... and so on. But clearly, in real life, if the errors are taken seriously and the cross-purposes are not discovered, the resulting situation is not so amusing. —Ed.

[33] It may be helpful for the modern reader to recall some synonyms for the verb "dominate:" control; manage; influence; handle; direct. The "drive to dominate" that Assagioli refers to may manifest itself in very subtle ways in a relationship, and most subtly, at times almost invisibly, in sexual relationships. —Ed.

these two drives — domination and sex. We may become aware of this but the awareness alone is not sufficient because the drive to dominate is so strong we have to work on it all the time. The Good Will comes in here — the giving up, willingly, [of] the dubious satisfaction of dominating and dictating. (1972 p. 2)

In this area, the most common mistakes are 1) criticism of others, 2) debates about who is wrong. That is fatal. It gets us nowhere ... all debate about "rightness" is futile because there is no perfect "right" or "wrong." 3) Another cause of trouble is expecting consistency in the other partner. This is a psychological mistake; no one is consistent, nor should they be. To be consistent is to be frozen — static. We are always changing and we cannot be consistent. It is foolish to ask it in a mate.[34] We should always try to change for the better. People feel it is not right to be expected to be consistent, but they do not know how to express it, so they get furious. When you give up [the expectation of] consistency, a great obstacle is eliminated. (1972 p. 2)

Pathology of the Couple

Let us now come to the pathology of the couple and then to the treatment and the integration. Stress has ... been put on sexual maladjustments. . . Sex is, of course, [being studied in a] highly scientific [way], and love is not. A very few — Havelock Ellis, Sorokin and Fromm — have begun to study love in a scientific way.... Sexual pathology cannot be healed on a purely biological level. Though some troubles can be healed on the

Sexual pathology cannot be healed on a purely biological level. Most sex troubles are psychosomatic.

---

[34] However, it is pertinent to recall that Assagioli had read Emerson, who wrote in his essay *Self-Reliance* that "a foolish consistency is the hobgoblin of little minds," with the intention, not to condemn *all* forms of consistency, but of unwarranted ones. Assagioli was a great advocate of personal growth and evolution, and knew that growth requires a break with what one has done, thought, or said in the past. —*Ed.*

physical plane through endocrinology. But most of the sex troubles are psychosomatic. (1957 p. 1)

Then there are the neurotic troubles. One cannot make a harmony out of two disharmonies. So first there must be harmonization of each on his [or her] own ground, and especially the elimination of those obstacles which, more directly, constitute stumbling blocks — specially the father and mother complexes. These are very well known . . . yet other complexes complicate the situation. "Insofar as a man is happily married to himself, he is fit for married life to another," said Novalis. This means: in a general way, that only so far as he is psychosynthesized within himself, and only so far as [a] man has recognized and has developed in himself a certain number of the feminine traits, can he be understanding of [a] woman — and vice-versa for the woman. Only if a man has a right understanding and appreciation, without idealism — objective, right understanding — towards womanhood (and vice versa for the woman) can he be happily married. (1957 pp. 1-2)

> One cannot make a harmony out of two disharmonies.
> "Insofar as a man is happily married to himself, he is fit for married life to another."
> — Novalis

The greatest obstacle to harmonious relationship can be put in non-scientific terms — and that is self-assertion. All too often, marriages are a battlefield for self-assertion. It cannot be completely eliminated, but it is often quite excessive. [Excessive selfassertion] is due to a conscious or unconscious sense of inferiority which leads to over-compensation, conflict between the sexes . . . All this should be closely psychoanalyzed before marriage and corrected as much as possible. (1957 p. 2)

> The greatest obstacle to harmonious relationship is self-assertion.

There are two rules for a happy marriage:

Psychosynthesis of the Couple

1. Not to demand that the partner is better than oneself. If one has fits of anger, one should not ask that the partner should have none, and vice versa. It is very simple to say this, but very difficult to put it into practice.

2. *Generosity.* The need for generosity was so well stressed by Hermann Keyserling. Previously, Duclos had very tersely expressed the same truth in this way: "One of the first social virtues is to tolerate in others what one has to refrain from in oneself." That is, we have to tolerate others being worse than ourselves. [35]

> First, justice; secondly, clear-sighted generosity —
> these are the two great pitfalls, stumbling-blocks
> and difficulties. (1957 p. 2)

Then there are the difficulties due to external factors. I will not deal with economic factors and social pressures, but only with the psychological factors due to the "in-laws," etc. All this sounds pretty gloomy, but luckily it is only "the [back] side of the medal." The first and most important thing is to give up the romantic, idealistic conception of marriage, expressed in the typical end-of-the-19th-century novels, where both lived happily ever after. That is one of the most untrue and harmful ideals. One has to enter marriage clear-sightedly, knowing that it is both a difficult and a beautiful undertaking. But this presupposes a general acceptance of conflicts, of pain, of tensions, as vital factors in life — giving up the spoiled-child psychological attitude, the "demanding" attitude to life. First, we accept this attitude, and

---

[35] From *Considérations sur les mœurs de ce siècle* by encyclopedist Charles Pinot Duclos (1704-1772) Clearly, Dr. Assagioli was here referring to more or less average, more or less healthy relationships. He does not say *how much* worse behavior can be for a partner to tolerate it. Modern studies have documented and studied different types and levels of abusive behavior in relationships, and it is safe to assume that abusive behavior was not included in Assagioli's advice on tolerance. He is clearly advocating a generous respect for individual differences. —*Ed.*

then, as one Oriental writer has said, "we grow through the presentation of a series of crises." (1957 p. 2)

Another convincing fact has been paradoxically but very wisely stated: "It is much more difficult to stand success than failure" — that is, favorable, harmonious factors can be fatal. Complacent, normal people who do not have the benefit of maladjustment in themselves, experience no growth, and do not contribute to humanity.[36] In this we see the value of "the shadow" aspect. There must be the acceptance of difficulties. Then, with this acceptance, you can enter into marriage. One does not then expect from marriage what it cannot give — i.e., a fool's paradise. (1957 p. 3)

> "We grow through the presentation of a series of crises."

The psychosynthesis of the couple . . . can be implemented in a satisfactory way only if it is framed or placed in a general conception of life that is understood and accepted by both spouses. This concept requires the elimination of two fundamental errors and illusions. (1965-3 p. 1)

The first is the search for pleasure and happiness as ends in themselves; that is, a hedonistic and selfish conception of life. But such ends can never be achieved, since suffering cannot be eliminated from life; any attempt to escape it, to push it back or rebel, only increases it. On the other hand, a willing acceptance and understanding of the useful and necessary function of suffering attenuates it, and can not only counterbalance it but also make it a source of joy. Here, perhaps a clarification is needed: to understand anything in psychology, one must always

---

[36] Assagioli's curious phrase "the benefit of maladjustment" here provides a window into his appreciation of the potential that can be derived from the difficulties and obstacles of life — provided that one responds positively and constructively to them. Many traditional teachings with which Assagioli was familiar and from which he drew inspiration, such as Sufism, stress that apparent "problems" are actually often gifts of life, if one can see them from the higher perspective. That perspective, of course, is an essential component of psychosynthesis. —*Ed.*

keep in mind the multiplicity of human nature, its various levels, the different subpersonalities that exist *simultaneously* inside us. So there can be suffering on one level and joy on another. They do not neutralize each other, they coexist; and in these cases it could be called a "peaceful coexistence." (1965-3 p. 1)

The second mistake or illusion is the search for stability, "security," for *static* harmony or peace. These cannot exist in human life, which by its very nature is fluid, dynamic, constantly evolving, as is cosmic life in all its manifestations. Stability, security, and peace exist and can be found, but only in a higher sphere of reality, in the transcendent where our true being, the spiritual Self dwells. But it is an illusion to seek that stability and peace in one's personal life, which includes various relationships with others. The spiritual Self lives in a sphere of reality that has laws and an essence completely different from those of the sphere of becoming, of changing, of evolution. (1965-3 p. 1)

Two fundamental errors and illusions: the search for pleasure and happiness as ends in themselves; and the search for stability, "security," for static harmony or peace.

Personal human life is essentially development, growth, and implementation of latent, superior possibilities. It is struggle and triumph, and therefore necessarily implies conflicts, tensions, overcoming, and alternations of joy and suffering — in addition to the possible coexistence which I have mentioned. When this is well-understood and accepted, the fundamental error of attributing fault — for the difficulties, the disharmonies and the travails that are inherent in life in the world, to external conditions or to other people — is avoided. (1965-3 pp. 1-2)

Life is struggle and triumph, and implies conflicts, tensions, overcoming, and alternations of joy and suffering.

One of the major obstacles to the implementation of the psychosynthesis of the couple, and one of the most common and most difficult to eliminate, is mutual blame. It manifests itself in the innumerable discussions about who is "right" and who is "wrong;" but this approach is totally misguided! It is not a question of "right" or "wrong," but of different points of view, appraisals, and accents. These are determined primarily by the different psychological constitution of man and woman in general; then, by the different psychological types; and also, by the individual peculiarities of each, and by their different experiences throughout life. This is part of the general principle, the fundamental truth, that in both the physical and psychic world there is nothing absolute; everything is relative. (1965-3 p. 2)

In the physical world, each phenomenon is relative in at least three ways: first, by its position in space; second, in the flow of time; third, according to the scale of dimensions and the orders of magnitude that the observer examines. The laws that apply at the molecular and atomic level are not applicable to the sub-atomic one. All modern physics has shown this. (1965-3 p. 2)

This relativity exists even more in the psychological field, and in more varied and complex ways. This was well highlighted by *"general semantics,"* which has demonstrated the non-applicability of Aristotelian logic with its "principle of the excluded middle." [37] [38] On this occasion I cannot go into technical

[37] General Semantics was first presented under that name by Alfred Korzybski in 1933 with the publication of *Science and Sanity: An Introduction to Non-Aristotelian Systems and General Semantics*, and advanced by others. According to this approach, things cannot be defined in the way that Greek philosopher Aristotle maintained, and therefore the polarities of Aristotelian logic are not valid descriptions of empirical reality.—*Ed.*

[38] In his *Metaphysics*, Aristotle gives a precise statement of what has been called *the law of excluded middle*: "since it is impossible that contradictories should be at the same time true of the same thing, obviously contraries also cannot belong at the same time to the same thing." (Book IV, Ch. 6). He then proposes that "there cannot be an intermediate between contradictories, but of one subject we must either affirm or deny any one predicate" (Book IV, Ch 7). This is the classic statement of "either/or" linear logic that Assagioli, along with many other modern thinkers, asserts is not able to adequately describe empirical reality. See *Basic Works of Aristotle*, edited by R. McKeon. New York, Random House, 1941. —*Ed.*

explanations, but I will clarify this point with a very simple analogy. According to the "excluded middle principle," an object is *either* white *or* black; a statement is *either* true *or* false; but — unfortunately for the logicians, and fortunately for those who feel the value of the wonderful variety of life — there is an indefinite series of grays, and numerous combinations of white or black areas can be made. (1965-3 p. 2)

Applying this to our theme, disputing the mutual "right" or "wrong" makes little sense and is of no use. The differences of opinions or appraisals and the consequent choices and decisions to be implemented must be examined objectively, serenely — I would say "scientifically." In this way, and only in this way, is it possible to reach a mutual understanding — an agreement with opportune reciprocal concessions, without any "winner" or "loser," and therefore a harmonious and fruitful cooperation. This applies to all sorts of problems, from spiritual and psychological to practical. (1965-3 p. 2)

In the physical world, each phenomenon is relative in space, in time, and in the dimensions used by the observer. The wonderful variety of life is not built of blacks and whites, but of an indefinite series of grays.

Love, Attraction, and Synthesis

[Now we consider some] *constructive aspects.* The first is the self-realization through the partner, that is, the development of the inferior and undeveloped dualities through the beneficent influence of the partner and, through the partner, of each human being. Through the other, each becomes more complete and is helped in his own individual psychosynthesis. Then comes the real *psychosynthesis of the couple* which can be divided into two aspects or levels — first, marriage as an art; secondly, marriage as a mission. Marriage as

The real psychosynthesis of the couple has two aspects or levels: marriage as an art, and marriage as a mission.

an art is based on love as an art, the art of loving. It is a romantic conception that love is spontaneous and that everybody knows how to love, as the mother who instinctively loves her child. Love is a fine art — perhaps the finest and wisest of all the human arts, and every art has a technique and a development from all levels — from the technique to the intellect and from the intellect to the intuition. (1957 p. 3)

Then, there is love as a mission — by the couple to the group. The couple which is wrapped up in each other forgets the rest of the world. Two egoists are worse than one! The symbol of the couple is an ellipse with two foci.[39] Then imagine two triangles, one with the apex upward, the other with the apex downwards. The downward triangle leads to the family, to the children. The *ideal* couple should be creative in two directions: The physical creation of children, which soon leads to educational psychology and educative creativity.[40]

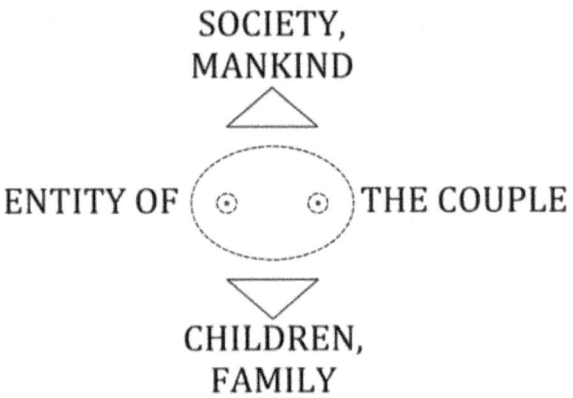

---

[39] This concept is drawn from Hermann Keyserling, who referred to the couple as analogous to an elliptical force field with two foci, in "The Correct Statement of the Marriage Problem," in *The Book of Marriage*. New York, Harcourt Brace & Co. 1926.

[40] I think it is clear that Assagioli's approach also applies to couples who do not produce biological children of their own; for the dynamics of all kinds and levels creativity within a family may draw out the couple's energy. —Ed.

Upwards to society and mankind: the creativity of the couple in society. And, finally, that there should be the mutual realization of the transcendent. (1957 p. 3)

A more differentiated and precise way of describing and examining these various relationships is one based on different bio-psychological functions and activities.

> 1. At the *biological level* there is physical, sexual attraction. It is a vast and currently much-discussed topic, but I cannot deal with it on this occasion. I will only say that sexual harmony and disharmony (in strictly the biological *sense*), certainly has considerable importance in the couple's psychosynthesis, but not the preponderant or almost exclusive one that many attribute to it, especially as a result of the spread of psychoanalytical doctrines. There are examples of couples who have implemented psycho-spiritual communion without, or despite the lack of, harmony in sexual relations, or after their ceasing sexual relations. Conversely, there are numerous couples with satisfactory physical relationships which are not enough to avoid serious conflicts. (1965-3 p. 5)

Four levels of bio-psychological functions and activities: biological, emotional, mental, and volitional (the field of the will)

> 2. Relationships on the *emotional level* would require an even longer discussion. In fact, they constitute the boundless theme of what is called "love." This is a word that is used in different and opposite ways. Here, too, I will have to limit myself to a few hints; that is, to indicate some of the types of emotional relationships that can most help or hinder the couple's psychosynthesis. There are in fact:
>
>> a. The love that could be called *"integrative,"* in which each of the two seeks, more or less consciously, what he or she lacks or aspires to. Maslow calls it *"love and belonging needs."* It includes passionate love and

romantic love. In its best aspects it produces a mutual integration, and therefore favors the psychosynthesis of the couple. But not infrequently it is a demanding, absorbent, and jealous love.

b. *Possessive* love. It has similarities with the previous type but it differs from it in that one who "loves" in this way does not seek integration with the loved person, but tries to *possess them for themselves*, to dominate them. In extreme cases this is actually not "love" but a manifestation of the "will to power." In America the type of woman who seeks this is called a "vamp," that is a "vampire"!

c. "*Oblational*" love, whose characteristics are devotion, dedication, willing sacrifice for the loved one, or for a superior Being. In the past, oblational love was a [common] characteristic of the Indian wife, who considered her husband to be her lord, her "guru" or spiritual instructor, and even a representative of God. Oblational and possessive love are often found in motherly love, combined in various proportions.

d. "*Radiant*" love. This type is unlike the "oblational" one, with which it could be confused. It does not consist in giving oneself (or something of oneself) to another being, but a pouring out of love to many or to all beings. It can have various features or specific qualities: fraternity, compassion, and communion.

These different types of love are not mutually exclusive, but, given the multiplicity of the human being, they can mix in various proportions and alternate in various times and ways. (1965-3 pp. 5-6)

3. In the *mental field*, mutual understanding is not easy, given the diverse ways men and women use the mind. This does not mean that the woman is less intelligent than the man —

as some people have erroneously asserted — but that she [often] uses her intelligence in a different way. In [what might be called] "undeveloped" women, the mind is dominated by feelings and emotions, and is placed at their service — but this also happens to many men! In [what could be called more] "highly developed" women, the mind is subordinated to intuition, whose insights it tries to grasp and interpret. On the other hand, a man [often] wants to use his mind as his sole instrument of knowledge. He seeks and finds — or deludes himself into thinking he has found — in his logical mind the motives that impel him into action. Generally [such a man] has no intuition, and therefore does not understand nor appreciate it in women. Knowing these differences can greatly help to reach an understanding. (1965-3 p. 6)

4. In the *field of the will*, interpersonal relationships have a great importance, both in general and particularly in married life, since they are often the cause of the most bitter conflicts that can lead to the dissolution of a marriage. These conflicts are produced by the tendency to self-affirmation, to domination, to the imposition of one's own will. Note that this is a tendency that exists in all people, and not only in the types who are constitutionally strong-willed and imperative. It also exists in weak people as a reaction or hyper-compensation for feelings of inferiority, or for a real deficiency. These conflicts can be mitigated and also resolved by frank recognition and a serene and in-depth examination of the problem by both partners, with the good will to solve it using suitable means. The mutual understanding in this sense can be implemented in two ways:

> a. *First*, by a clear separation of the "fields" of dominance and authority in family life. These distinctions are natural, and, therefore with good will, agreement on them can be reached without too much difficulty.
>
> b. *Second*, by an appropriate alternation of assertive and accommodating attitudes [on the part of each

partner]. It is good to keep in mind, in these situations, the psychological mechanism that could be called "shifting the target," or "target displacement." For example, when a mother is unhappy or exasperated by the behavior of her children or the maid, she often discharges her irritation on her husband when he returns home! Conversely, [for example], a husband who has suffered abuse or humiliation in the office or in another work situation often discharges his repressed irritation onto his wife. If you are able to remember and be convinced in such situations that *in reality* your spouse does not at all "have it in for you," and if, therefore, you manage not to react or argue, everything will be over after such a "discharge," and indeed a surge of affection can take over. This emotional "game of forces" has been acutely described by Laura Archera Huxley, wife of the writer Aldous Huxley who recently passed away, in her book entitled *You Are Not the Target*.[41] It is a book full of humor and gives witty and original practical advice on the art of living. (1965-3 pp. 6-7)

The alternation of attitudes in this type of relationship can be consciously regulated by coming to an agreement in moments of calm and mutual understanding. Thus, the spouses can agree to be assertive and "discharging," or accommodating and "receptive," at different moments of the day; or, as an American couple has proposed and implemented, on alternate days (except Sunday, considered to be a day of truce and equal communion!). (1965-3 p. 7)

Then there is another difference in the relationships, of which the spouses should have a clear awareness: the difference between the three attitudes and functions that each man and woman have, and which can be considered as sub-personalities. In a man there are the *filial* (son) attitude and the *conjugal* (husband) and *fatherly* functions; correspondingly in a woman

---

[41] New York, Farrar Strauss, republished in 1998 by Da Capo Lifelong Books

there are the *filial* (daughter) attitude and the *conjugal* (wife) and *maternal* functions. In the normal evolution of life, the filial "personality" appears first, then the conjugal one, to which are added the paternal or maternal ones. I said "added," since the earlier attitudes and functions remain to varying degrees throughout one's life. Here too there are typological differences. For example, there are women in whom the conjugal function clearly predominates and the maternal function is deficient, while in other women the opposite occurs. (1965-3 p. 7)

> *Three attitudes or subpersonalities in men and women toward each other in a couple: filial, conjugal, and parental.*

But in addition to these differences that are more or less permanent or gradually evolving, there is often a rapid alternation between the three attitudes, depending on the circumstances and life events. There are times when a man or a woman feels inclined to abandon themselves to their partner in a childlike way and ask their help. At other times, they feel impelled to behave with their spouse in a paternal or maternal way. A clear knowledge of these alternations and rhythms, and their conscious and agreed upon implementation, is one of the most important tasks of the art of "living together." (1965-3 p. 7)

All this helps to eliminate many unnecessary disagreements and creates the conditions for the implementation of the couple's psychosynthesis. On the positive side, the two essential qualities for this psychosynthesis are: loving understanding and the *spirit of cooperation*. They are necessary in all interpersonal relationships, but particularly in those between a man and a woman. There can be no order, harmony, or social peace if these qualities do not exist in individuals, and especially in the family. (1965-3 pp. 7-8)

[On the other hand,] it may happen that an individual seeks to lose oneself in the couple, to lose one's personality by merging entirely in the other: this is a romantic ideal that we can call regressive, and which has been illustrated notably by the story of Tristan and Isolde. It naturally leads to suicide, because it is impossible to lose oneself entirely in one's beloved. This is a false interpretation of a true intuition: to be delivered from the limits of the personality. The mistake is to try to achieve this fusion only on the emotional and physical plane, because true and total union are possible only on the plane of the soul. (N.D.1 p. 2)

It is impossible to lose oneself entirely in one's beloved. True and total union are possible only on the plane of the soul.

One great cause of difficulty is the fundamental ambivalence.[42] There are many ambivalences in each of us. They have been pointed out but have not been given enough emphasis. Any impact of a situation is apt to arouse an ambivalent reaction. Then there is the *multiplicity* of reactions caused by the different subpersonalities. We are a multiplicity of subpersonalities, each wanting its own way. When both partners are psychologically sophisticated they can play with them and consciously deal with them, and in frank conversation admit the problems. For example, one partner says, "This is your childish personality. You can do better," or "I think this is an image of your father." So, if both are sophisticated, and are of good will, much can be explained and [resolved]. There must be a constant watchfulness.
(1972 p. 3)

Another point: I'm going back to [the] recognition of the other as an individual, which is well emphasized by Martin Buber in *I and Thou*. A good example of graciously agreeing to disagree is that of Elizabeth and Robert Browning, one of the best examples of psychosynthesis of the couple. They had love for each other,

---

[42] It may be that Assagioli is using this term in its classic psychoanalytic meaning. Ambivalence is defined in the International Dictionary of Psychoanalysis as "the simultaneous presence of conflicting feelings and tendencies with respect to an object." It seems likely that Assagioli is calling attention to peoples' common diversity and ambiguity of motivations and drives, which of course, if they are not congruent, can cause difficulties between people. He also seems to be suggesting that ambivalence of one kind or another is a basic quality of human beings.—*Ed.*

and many common activities, but they also had individual activities. She went to séances and he didn't approve but he didn't interfere, though he disagreed.[43] The point is to let the other do things which we don't like. This brings up the question, which often comes up when one is spiritually inclined and the partner is not, or may be antagonistic to it. This is difficult but can be dealt with. This difficulty is based generally on the difference of evolutionary stages and inner maturity.[44] The less developed one is not at fault and must be accepted. The more evolved one should be more understanding and generous and should refrain from talking to the partner about these things. The partner is not ready and should be given time to be prepared. Meditation and study should be kept to oneself. One can say, "This is my hobby, but there are worse hobbies like collecting expensive items. You are free to have *your* hobbies." Say this with no superior attitude, but not renouncing your own life. Moreover, one can be more mature on one level and less mature on another, e.g. mature intellect but primitive emotions, or vice-versa. When the partner is hostile consider this as a life difficulty that we need in order to grow. (1972 p. 3)

Ways to Agreement and Synthesis

The basic attitude [that is needed] is the recognition, acceptance and respect of the other as *a human being in his [or her] own right*. This may seem obvious, but we don't do it! We want others to be as we wish them to be, but again, this is nonsense. Respect for individuals in [their] own right is the basis of mutual freedom. On this basis one can deal intelligently with differences and

---

[43] This example may have been of personal significance for Assagioli, because his wife Nella was much more enthusiastic about spiritualism and séances than he was, although he certainly did not "disapprove" of them. —*Ed.*

[44] Roberto Assagioli's entire life's work was centered around the development of human beings. His emphasis on synthesis and education were only two of the facets of psychosynthesis, but were emblematic of his desire to do work that allowed people to grow and mature at every possible level. As part of this work he routinely observed peoples' progress toward their psychosynthesis, and the words "evolutionary stages" and "maturity" are among those he would use to gauge peoples' work and progress. —*Ed.*

Psychosynthesis of the Couple

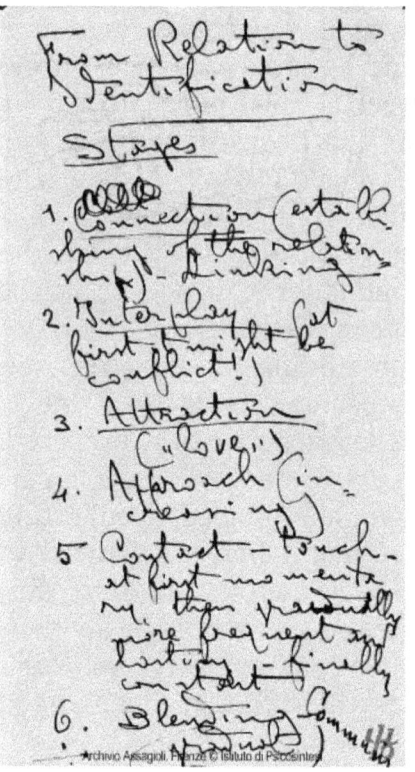

Hand-written Notes from the Assagioli Archives Doc.#8565

From Relation to Identification - Stages.

1. Connection (establishing of the relationship). Linking.
2. Interplay (at first it might be conflict!).
3. Attraction ("love")
4: Approach (increasing)
5. Contact - touch - at first momentary,
   then gradually more frequent and lasting -
   finally constant
6. Blending (gradual), Communion — Unification
   a) in consciousness
   b) in action.
   Cooperation
7. Unity. Identification

real disagreements. So the first thing is to "agree to disagree." People sometimes sentimentally try to agree but it is artificial. Disagreements should be allowed; it is part of the existential condition. It is the starting point for mutual adjustment, concessions and right compromise. Of course, this will be different in each case. It is summed up by the saying used by a monastic order, "In what is necessary — unity; in what is doubtful — freedom; in everything — spiritual love (*caritas*)." But, what is necessary? Very, very few things are really necessary. Then there is a further step: we can recognize and utilize the differences. It would really be tiresome if we were all alike. Therefore, the task is how to utilize the mutual integration of differences in the psychosynthesis of the couple and make a rich unity composed of integrated different polarities and differences. All this requires a basic good will, a loving attitude in spite of the imperfections of the other. Blind passionate love is unrealistic and brings disillusionment, but it is not as common as in the past. We are more critical and analytical. Good will and love lead to understanding, to understanding each other. (1972 p. 3)

We cannot accurately speak of women and men in general. Each one of us is a human being before being "man" or "woman." And each one of us, man or woman, has roles and functions to fulfill, individually, inter-individually and socially. Here is where the differences begin. These are most emphatically not differences in *value*, only differences in *function*. The human being is never defined by any of these roles. [For example] women, as human beings, can accept or not accept the role of wife or of mother. She can choose another vocation. It is not a "must," a necessity. It is a free choice. (1974a p. 2)

Each one of us is a human being before being "man" or "woman."

Woman therefore is right in demanding that she be treated as a human being and not as a "mere woman," as simply a woman and only that. She is right for refusing to be identified with a certain image of woman. She is a living being, with all the dignity and the potential of a whole human being. All attitudes which

Psychosynthesis of the Couple

limit the possibilities of woman are mistaken. Women have the right to demand respect and parity with men. And the same, of course, is true for men. (1974a p. 2)

Each of us can equally choose to play different roles. For instance, a woman can decide to play the role of spouse or of mother, or both. She can carry on a creative, social or business activity. She can choose one role, or she can alternate several of them, perhaps during the same day, perhaps over longer periods of time. This is the free choice of a human being. I believe in the primacy of the human being unconditioned by his or her sex. (1974a p. 2)

The differences between men and women are clearly found reflected in our environment — in the family and in society — and it is here that we must work to eliminate their unfair and harmful crystallization into rigid stereotypes and prejudices. (1974a p. 2)

But it is important to realize that these differences exist also within our psyche, in the depths of our unconscious, and, just as much, in the collective unconscious of humanity, where they appear through some of the most powerful archetypes. So there are universal masculine and feminine principles, which manifest themselves in quite diverse ways through different individuals. In other words, while masculine and feminine principles do exist in the universe, different people experience them and describe them in different ways — as is equally the case with beauty, truth, harmony, goodness, justice or any of the other universal principles. (1974a pp. 2-3)

> *There are universal masculine and feminine principles, which manifest in diverse ways through different individuals.*

The point is not to try to define what these principles are, but to distinguish, in our consciousness and in our relations with others, "masculine" and "feminine" from "man" and "woman." We need to recognize that both the masculine and feminine principles exist in their own right, and that they are present —

although in unique forms and different proportions — in every man and in every woman. (1974a p. 3)

Within each human being is a percentage of psychological masculinity and a percentage of psychological femininity, completely independent of the sex of the individual. Each person is a unique combination of these energies. When we look at women on the whole, we find that they are more attuned to the feminine principle, have greater access to it and have a greater percentage of it in their psychological makeup. And similarly, men are more attuned to the masculine principle. Of course this is a generality. People are unique. Some men are psychologically more feminine than many women, for instance. (1974a p. 3)

Take the example of the French novelist George Sand (the pen name of Madame DuDevant) and Chopin. They were lovers, and he, physically, had the "man" role and she the "woman" role. But psychologically he was feminine and she was masculine. She talked like a man, wrote in a vigorous style — and smoked cigars! In her personality, masculinity predominated, while Chopin was imaginative, sensitive.

There is therefore a difference between physical sex and psychological characteristics. Over the years, I have met many who feared — or even believed — themselves to be homosexuals just because they did not recognize this distinction.[45] (1974a p. 3)

---

[45] The four references in Assagioli's notes in the Archives relating to homosexuality include document #15909 which includes it in a list of "individual maladjustments;" and document #15611, that ponders whether the alternation of masculine and feminine incarnations may be reasons for some kinds of homosexuality. The other two include a quote from Freud and a comment that the "The Bisexual Androgyne" of the "Integrated Human Being" is "not homosexual." Assagioli died (in 1974) before homosexual rights and same-sex marriage became social issues and before they were accepted by many, if not all, modern societies. Nevertheless this paragraph was included in one of his last writings, suggesting that, as a therapist, he was fully aware of the issues of gender identity and sexual orientation. As he kept up with current events in the world of psychology, he was probably aware of recent developments in the approaches to sex and gender among the international psychological community. —*Ed.*

Only by accepting both the masculine and feminine principles, bringing them together, and harmonizing them within ourselves, we will be able to transcend the conditioning of our roles, and to express the whole range of our latent potential. [46] (1974a p. 3)

The will is not merely assertive, aggressive and controlling. There is the accepting will, the yielding will, the dedicated will. You might say that there is a feminine polarity to the will — the willing surrender, the joyful acceptance of the other functions of the personality. I can state the same point in another way. At the heart of the self there is both an active and a passive element, an agent and a spectator. Self-consciousness involves our being a witness — a pure, objective, loving witness — to what is happening within and without. In this sense the self is not a dynamic in itself but is a point of witness, a spectator, an observer who watches the flow. But there is another part of the inner self — the will-er or the directing agent — that actively intervenes to orchestrate the various functions and energies of the personality, to make commitments and to instigate action in the external world. So, at the center of the self there is a unity of masculine and feminine, will and love, action and observation. (1974b p.5)

It is not at all a question of superiority or inferiority. Masculine and feminine psychological characteristics, even though dissimilar, are of the same value. This is a statement of fact.
(1974a p. 4)

A controversial question is whether the fact that women frequently have certain functions better developed and men others is the product of nature, or of education, or of social pressure. In my opinion all three factors are present, in different proportions, in each individual. While this is an important social problem, fortunately, from the individual's standpoint it can be largely sidestepped. He or she need only consider how he or she is right now, and how he or she can improve. (1974a p. 4)

---

[46] See Appendix A for Assagioli's writing on the Balancing and Synthesis of the Opposites.

Psychosynthesis of the Couple

The psychosynthesis of the individual requires that the elements of the opposite sex existing in him or in her be recognized and developed in their higher aspects, and integrated, albeit in a subordinate way, into a complete personality. But it is essential that the *higher* aspects are developed, since it is easier for the lower ones to be manifested, that is, masculinized women and effeminate men — and this often happens. This integration of each individual is facilitated, indeed implemented spontaneously to some extent, by their living together. (1965-3 p. 8)

If a woman has had fewer opportunities or incentives to express her ideas, her thoughts, it does not seem to me to be necessary to spend much time and energy to search to understand why, who is responsible for this, and so forth. Quite simply, if this function is insufficiently developed, she can develop it. And the same is true for a man who has not developed his feelings, or his intuition. (Needless to say, there are men who need to develop their intellect, and women who need to get in touch with their feelings and cultivate their intuition). The point is to recognize the strong qualities and the deficiencies — and to bring them into a condition of harmony and balance. This is what I call a psychologically and spiritually practical approach.
(1974a pp. 4-5)

A couple [whose relationship is] founded on a basis of fundamental equality, respect, reciprocal appreciation as human beings, can work out the psychosynthesis of their particular couple [relationship] together. Each one can work on his [or her] own psychosynthesis, and each one can also collaborate in the psychosynthesis of the other, helping the other to achieve his[or her] own psychosynthesis by helping him[or her] strengthen his[or her] less developed functions. Then once they have done this to a certain point, they can truly act as a couple by combining and complementing their qualities and functions in all situations: in their marriage, their role as parents, and in their social activities.
(1974a p. 5)

For each function to be developed training is needed — often including specific exercises. The process is analogous to the training of muscles: if one wants to play a certain sport, he finds someone who is competent, gets trained and afterwards continues to train himself. If a man recognizes that his emotional and imaginative sides have been neglected, he can cultivate them. If a woman finds that her mind is not as active as she would like, she can train it. One has to "cultivate one's garden" by planting different flowers. A woman or a man can do it alone, but it is often more effective, much easier and more enjoyable to do it together as two people. (1974a p. 5)

When we come to particular problems, many difficulties may emerge, and in each specific case we can apply a therapy. I speak of 'therapy' here in the broadest sense of the word, because none of us is one hundred percent healthy in the higher psychosynthetic sense. In difficult situations a benevolent and wise therapist or counselor can be of great assistance: someone impartial, kindly, comprehensive, who helps the two members of the couple to become more aware, who explains the situation, who indicates possible solutions and helps to choose the means to attain them. (1974a p. 5)

For each couple the situation is different. Each human being is unique. Thus unique multiplied by unique gives "unique squared;" this is a fundamental principle of psychosynthesis. Each case is unique, each situation is unique. Each couple is unique. Each family is unique. We need to focus on the unique existential problem of a certain situation, rather than on generalities, and afterwards to choose techniques which are most adequate for resolving the problems of that particular case. This eliminates the fictitious, inauthentic problems. It may be called the psychoanalytical phase — the discovery of the obstacles to constructive work. And the obstacles are for the most part those which we spoke about before: erroneous attitudes of men and women. I believe therefore in the equality of value, and in the differentiation of functions up to a certain point — collaboration, integration on a base of equality. (1974a pp. 5-6)

We are now in a period of crisis and profound changes. I believe that woman is evolving perhaps more rapidly than man. For him, the task is to discover the real human being beneath masculine limitations — to be not only a "masculine man," but a human being, who plays masculine roles, and if he chooses, feminine ones. We know that historically there were matriarchal civilizations and patriarchal civilizations; the ideal would be a new synthetic civilization, that is neither patriarchal nor matriarchal, but one that is psychosynthetic, that is to say, a civilization in which the highest and best qualities of each are manifested. (1974a p. 6)

The obstacles to constructive work are mostly erroneous attitudes of men and women.

This would be something new. In all historical civilizations and cultures there has been a preponderance of one or the other element. But in this new civilization and the emerging global culture, for the first time, humanity is sufficiently developed to make a planetary, global pattern, incorporating the very best of all men and women. I think that this planetary psychosynthesis, this psychosynthesis of humanity is possible and needed. Each particular problem will then have its frame of reference in the greater whole, and conflict can be replaced by harmonious integration and cooperation. All of this is within our reach — for not only is it very beautiful — it is very human. (1974a p. 6)

Humanity is sufficiently developed to make a global pattern, incorporating the very best of all men and women. The psychosynthesis of humanity is possible and needed.

Reference Sources

Assagioli 1957: Transcript of a talk in English titled "Psychosynthesis of the Couple," given by Roberto Assagioli, MD, at Capolona, Italy, May 16, 1957.

Assagioli 1958: Transcript of a talk in English titled "Inter-Individual Psychosynthesis," given by Roberto Assagioli, MD, at a Conference at the Valmy Estate in Delaware, USA, hosted by the Psychosynthesis Research Foundation, May 23-25, 1958.

Assagioli 1965-1: Transcript of a lecture in Italian titled "La Coppia Umana," Lesson V in a Course of Lessons on Psychosynthesis, given by Roberto Assagioli, MD, at Casa Assagioli, Firenze, Italy, February 14, 1965; translated from the Italian as "The Human Couple" by Catherine Ann Lombard.

Assagioli 1965-2: Transcript of Lecture VIII titled "Dalla Coppia alla Communità Umana" From a Course of Lessons on Psychosynthesis, given in Italian by Roberto Assagioli, MD, at Casa Assagioli, Firenze, Italy, given March 21, 1965, translated by Jan Kuniholm.

Assagioli 1965-3: Transcript of a lecture in Italian titled "La Psicosintesi nel Matrimonio," given by Roberto Assagioli, MD, at Casa Assagioli, Firenze, Lesson VII in a Course of Lessons on Psychosynthesis at Casa Assagioli, Firenze, Italy, March 14, 1965; translated from the Italian as "Psychosynthesis in

	Marriage" by Catherine Ann Lombard and Jan Kuniholm.
Assagioli 1968	"The Psychology of Woman and Her Psychosynthesis," was published in Italian as "La psicologia della donna e la sua psicosintesi", in *L'economia umana*, 9, 11, 1958. The first English edition was originally published in *Psychics International Vol. II: 2, pp. 58-61, August 1965*. This English version was prepared by Frank Haronian, PhD, with the cooperation and approval of Roberto Assagioli and published by The Psychosynthesis Research Foundation in 1968.
Assagioli 1972:	Transcript of a talk in English titled "Psychosynthesis of the Couple," by Roberto Assagioli, MD, (and edited by Dr. Assagioli from the original transcript) given in Italy August 18, 1972.
Assagioli 1974a:	"A Higher View of the Man-Woman Problem," by Roberto Assagioli, MD, and Claude Servan-Schreiber. Published in English in *Synthesis,* Volume 1 (1974, and re-published 1977) pages 116-123. This article consisted of introductory remarks by Servan-Schreiber followed by extended quotations from Assagioli.
Assagioli 1974b:	"The Golden Mean of Roberto Assagioli," An interview conducted with Dr. Assagioli by Sam Keen that was published in the December 1974 issue of *Psychology Today*.

Assagioli N.D.1: Undated Document #16008 from the Assagioli Archives in Florence, Italy, titled "La Psychosinthèse du Couple, Transcrit à partir d'un manuscript," translated from the French as "Psychosynthesis of the Couple" by Jan Kuniholm.

Assagioli N.D.2: Undated transcript of a talk in English titled "The Human Couple" given by Roberto Assagioli, MD, from a series of lectures on Inter-individual psychosynthesis. From the Assagioli Archives, Florence, Italy.

Additional Bibliography

Assagioli, Roberto, *The Act of Will.* Woking, England, UK, David Platts Publishing Company, 1999.

Assagioli, Roberto, *Psychosynthesis: A Collection of Basic Writings.* Amherst, MA, USA. The Synthesis Center, 2000.

Assagioli, Roberto, *Transpersonal Development.* Findhorn, Scotland, UK. Inner Way Productions, 2007.
(Note: there are other editions of these books available)

Other writings of Roberto Assagioli may be found at:
http://www.psicosintesi.it/english
https://www.archivioassagioli.org/
https://kennethsorensen.dk/
https://www.psicoenergetica.it/

APPENDIX A:

Selected quotations from
THE BALANCING AND SYNTHESIS OF THE OPPOSITES
by Roberto Assagioli, M.D.
New York, Psychosynthesis Research Foundation, 1972.

In the physical world, the most commonly recognized polarity is that between the positive and negative poles in electricity. This polarity is the basis of the constitution of matter since, as is well known, each atom contains charges of electricity differentiated into a positive nucleus and a varying number of negative electrons. Electric polarity manifests itself in various ways which have many practical applications, as in induced and alternating currents, etc. Interesting analogies can be found in various polarities in the field of psychology, such as emotional attraction and repulsion, ambivalence and the "compensatory" function.

Within living organisms, such as the human body, there are various polarities. One of the most important is that between the sympathetic and the parasympathetic nervous systems; the former stimulates catabolism, the latter assimilation or anabolism. Other polarities exist between the different endocrine glands.

One of the most important and general polarities in the three kingdoms of organic life (vegetable, animal and human) is the sexual. The positive pole is represented by the masculine element, the negative by the feminine element. This does not mean that the former is active and the latter passive. Both are active, but in a different way, the masculine element being the dynamic, initiating pole, while the feminine element is the receptive, "gestative," elaborative pole. This type of polarity extends far beyond the man-woman relationship to innumerable manifestations in life. It has been particularly and deeply emphasized by the Chinese who regard these two principles as the foundation both of cosmic evolution and of every aspect of human life. The creative aspect, symbolized by the father and Heaven, they call Yang, while Yin is the receptive and elaborative aspect, symbolized by the mother and the Earth.[47] The well-being of Man depends, in the view of Chinese philosophy, on the harmonious accord between Man and the cyclic evolution of the Universe, woven from the innumerable relationships and interactions of Yang and Yin.[48] (p. 2)

There are also many "inter-individual" polarities which are of the utmost importance. The first and fundamental one is that existing, on all levels, between Man and Woman. Then there is that between adults and young people, particularly in the interaction between parents and their children. There are, further, the various relationships between individuals and the different groups to which they belong. Among them we find the family considered as a unit, as a "psychic entity," which is made up not only of members who are alive, but also of ancestral influences and family traditions. Such influences are sometimes a help to the individual, offering him an ideal and a way of life which he may be encouraged to live by. Other times, and perhaps more often, they may hem him in and even oppress him. (p. 3)

In the biological realm, health can be defined as a dynamic equilibrium ever threatened and ever restored between a series of polarities, such as exist between the divisions of the nervous system, between various endocrine glands, and in general between the anabolic and catabolic functions. In the same way, *psychological life* can be regarded as a *continual polarization and tension between differing tendencies and functions, and as a continual effort, conscious or not, to establish equilibrium.* Among

---

[47] See Appendices B and C below. —*Ed.*
[48] Numerous Chinese texts deal with this point. One of the most interesting is the *I Ching* or *The Book of Transformations*, which, disguised under the form of a method of divination, contains treasures of wisdom. Jung, in *The Secret of the Golden Flower*, and also Keyserling, expressed great appreciation of it. — *original note by R.A.*

the most important psychological polarities are: impulse-inhibition; feeling-reason; extraversion-introversion. (p. 5)

In sexual polarity, the union of the two physical elements has a creative effect. The dynamism of their fusion brings about the birth of a new organism similar to that of the parents. In humanity this wonderful physical creative function is closely associated with the *psychological* polarities, and this often produces very complex situations and difficult problems. (p. 5)

APPENDIX B:

"Yin and Yang"

In Ancient Chinese philosophy, **yin and yang** . . . is a Chinese philosophical concept that describes how obviously opposite or contrary forces may actually be complementary, interconnected, and interdependent in the natural world, and how they may give rise to each other as they interrelate to one another. In Chinese cosmology, the universe creates itself out of a primary chaos of material energy, organized into the cycles of Yin and Yang and formed into objects and lives. Yin is the receptive and Yang the active principle, seen in all forms of change and difference such as the annual cycle (winter and summer), the landscape (north-facing shade and south-facing brightness), sexual coupling (female and male), the formation of both men and women as characters and sociopolitical history (disorder and order).

Source: https://en.wikipedia.org/wiki/Yin_and_yang
Accessed 6/8/2021.

APPENDIX C:

Quotations from "Gender in Chinese Philosophy" in *Internet Encyclopedia of Philosophy*

The concept of gender is foundational to the general approach of Chinese thinkers. *Yin* and *yang*, core elements of Chinese cosmogony, involve correlative aspects of "dark and light," "female and male," and "soft and hard." These notions, with their deeply-rooted gender connotations, recognize the necessity of interplay between these different forces in generating and carrying forward the world ... The genders, in terms of social roles, are not defined absolutely or theoretically, but rather through the mutually reciprocal, physical, generative relationship between male and female. They are understood correlatively, and determined by their context and dynamic tendencies as they interact with one another ... The specific traits of the objects can only be designated *yin* and *yang* in their functional correlation to one another ... In this way, the early association of *yin* and *yang* with gender can be seen as speaking to the relationship between genders, and not to their essential or substantial natures. *Yin* and *yang* traits were thus seen as able to accurately describe broad differences between males and females as they interact with one another. Fixing the link between these categorizations, having men be *yang* in relation to women, who are *yin*, only works in a highly abstract or broad sense.

Source: "Gender in Chinese Philosophy" by Lijuan Shen, Xi'an University of Architecture and Technology, China and Paul D'Ambrosio, East China Normal University.
https://iep.utm.edu/gender-in-chinese-philosophy/
Accessed 6/30/2021.

Psychosynthesis of the Couple

An Uncommon Couple
Memories of Nella and Roberto Assagioli
A Reminiscence by Piero Ferrucci

I got to know Nella, Roberto Assagioli's wife, only during the last four years of her life. She was always courteous with me. When I was invited to lunch, she always insisted that I drink the wine, of which she was very proud. Roberto did not drink at all.

Roberto worked in his own home, and she was around, so at times I could see how the two of them interacted. Roberto was always extremely kind and considerate with her, with a sense of warmth and protection. I remember especially one episode. Roberto was dictating to me an article that was very important to him. It was about the transpersonal. He was visibly tired, and his voice was giving him some problems. However, he wanted to get it done. He was concentrating on each phrase he was dictating. I could see he had the whole article in his mind, ready to be written. Still, it was an effort. At this point the door suddenly opened and Nella came in: "Robertino, will you come and entertain my lady friends?" She was with a few of her friends, and wanted him to come and be part of the gathering. But at this time her dementia was already in progress. Roberto had very good "vibes"; if he just entered a room everybody would suddenly feel happy; it was an amazing capacity. Nella knew that.

Nella and Roberto Assagioli
c. 1970

But Roberto would have preferred not to be interrupted in his work. I was curious to see how he would handle it. I could perceive in his eyes a moment of hesitation. Then he said: "All right!" interrupted our work, sent me home, and went to entertain the old ladies. The point is, he always gave first priority to relationship, even more than to ideas and work. It was a very good lesson for me.

Another time, Roberto was in the mountains, in Badia Prataglia, where he sometimes went for the summer to escape the heat of Florence. I was doing my military service, which happened to be, of all places, very close to there. I was invited for lunch. Suddenly Carmela, their faithful waitress, came in with a cake, a many layered custard cake: "Dottore, le nozze d'oro!" The golden anniversary! Fifty years! Roberto looked a bit surprised. He knew, but had momentarily forgotten. Nella was already not quite herself. This was 1971, two years before her death. With just a few words, Roberto recalled their fifty years together, joys and sorrows, persecutions (it was the only time I ever heard him pronounce that word), the loss of their only son, but also many happy times together. And he recited by heart a short Italian poem, which I have tried to find ever since, without success. It was mainly about mutual support through the vicissitudes of life.

Nella died two years later. I was not there, but arrived shortly afterward. Ida Palombi, Roberto's secretary, told me he had big tears in his eyes. Somehow at the time I could not imagine him crying: that was not part of my image of a wise person. Now it is.

I would like at this point to say a word on how Roberto envisaged man and woman, and the couple. We know he had written about woman as "the queen of the house." In September of 1973 Betty Friedan, author of the seminal book *The Feminine Mystique*, and leading American feminist, came to visit Roberto as part of a group. Sometimes the group would see him, other times they would be with me, and I would guide them in a psychosynthesis exercise. Betty Friedan was quite interested. Once she had an intense experience when she visualized man and woman at the two ends of a rainbow, and united by the rainbow. This was a poetic image of peace between the sexes. At the end, the group was ready to leave. Roberto asked Ida Palombi to prepare some of his booklets, to give to Betty Friedan. I quickly and surreptitiously went to Ida and told her, "Whatever publication you give her, please do *not* include *The Psychology of Woman and her Psychosynthesis*—it's too old-fashioned and does not represent Assagioli anymore." After a few minutes Ida came in, walked directly to Betty Friedan with a pile of booklets. And guess which one was on top? Ida had her own strong ideas. God bless her and the enormous and precious work she did through the years for Roberto Assagioli. But we never heard from Betty Friedan again.

At one time I told Roberto I did not quite agree with his ideas about woman. He said he had changed his mind: "Once in a while one can change one's mind, no?" His idea was that the guiding principle in relating to both men and women was to think of them, first of all, as a Self, a being above role and gender and the flow of time. The Self is neither male nor female. So that took care of the *regina della casa.* He expressed these ideas in the interview with Claude Servan-Schreiber, published in the journal *Synthesis* in 1974. However, he told me, the couple will undergo a time of difficulties and adaptations for the next 150 years. I don't know where he got that figure. Since then we have gone almost 50 years.

A hundred more to go. (2021)

Index

A

acceptance 31, 54-55, 66, 71
Active 4, 16, 30, 41-42, 71, 73, 78, 80
Act of Will, The 10, 13
active 28, 41
Adler, Alfred 21
ambivalence 65, 78
American Psychological Association iv
analysis 25, 37, 48
anima, animus 38
archive iii, 15, 20, 22, 37, 45, 67, 70, 77
Assagioli, Nella vii, 3-4, 66, 82-83
assertion 11, 12, 18, 51, 53
attitude 38, 54, 63, 64, 66, 68
attraction vi, 28-29, 32, 33, 35, 41, 50, 58, 60, 67, 78
authority 11, 36-37, 62
awareness 9, 10, 43, 52, 63
Ayurvedic 9

B

balance 31, 36-37, 72
belief 46
bisexuality 38
blending 33, 67
Book of Marriage, The 18, 21, 59
Browning, Robert & Elizabeth 65
Buber, Martin 65
Bucke, R. Maurice 21

C

centers 25, 35-36

chakra 9
changes 2, 17, 50-51, 74
children 3, 12, 34, 36-37, 43, 45, 59, 63, 79
Chinese vii, 16, 78-81
choice 17, , 58, 68, 69
Chopin, Frederic 70
coherence 26, 35
communication vi, 49-50
communion 9, 25, 46-47, 50, 60, 61, 63
complementary 38-40, 80
conscious 2, 9, 26, 35, 38-41, 44, 48, 50, 53, 64, 79
consciousness 26, 35-36, 67, 69, 71
consistency 5, 52
consistent 6, 52
constitution 25, 38, 45, 57, 78
control 12, 26, 36-37, 51
correction 47
couple i-iii, vi-vii, 1, 3, 4, 6, 11, 12, 16-20, 22-25, 27-28, 31-37, 39-40, 45-48, 52, 55, 56, 58-60, 63-65, 68, 72-73, 75-77, 83, 84
crisis, crises iv-v, 54, 55, 74
criticism 52

D

D'Ambra, Lucio 21
D'Ambrosio, Paul 81
daughter 23, 63
debates 52
detachment 28, 41, 50
development iv, 4, 5, 10, 17, 31, 38-39, 56, 58, 59, 66

differences vi, 12, 16, 17, 29-31, 41-42, 50, 54, 58, 62, 64, 66, 68-69, 81
differential vi, 27
disposition 42
dominate 11, 51-52, 61, 62
Duclos, Charles Pinot 54
DuDevant, Madame 70,

Friedan, Betty 83-84
Fromm, Eric 52
functions 12-14, 27, 28, 30, 37, 39-41, 43, 60, 63-64, 68, 71-73, 79
fundamental 15, 25, 28-29, 35, 39, 41, 55-57, 65, 72, 73, 79

E

education 34, 36, 37, 45, 66, 71
electricity 78
Ellis, Havelock 52
Emerson, Ralph Waldo 52
emotional 8, 11, 13, 14, 23, 28-30, 33, 35-36, 38, 40, 42, 47, 50, 60, 63, 65, 73, 78
energy 8-10, 25, 36, 59, 72, 80
entity 18, 35-37, 40, 79
evidence 4-5
evolution 2, 12, 52, 56, 64, 79
expectation 52
external 40-41, 54, 56, 71
extroverts, extroversion 41-42

F

faith 46
family 4, 12, 42, 59, 62, 64, 69, 73, 79
father 23, 37, 43, 51, 53, 65, 79
feminine vi, 14-17, 29, 37-39, 43-44, 51, 53, 69-71, 74, 78, 83
feminine principle vi, 15-17, 29, 69-71
feminist 39, 83
Florence, Italy ii, iii, 6, 14, 21, 77, 83
Freud, Sigmund 2, 70

G

gender vii, 39, 41, 43, 70, 81, 84
generosity 54
Giovetti, Paola 4

H

habits 28
happiness 55, 56
Harding, M. Esther 21
harmony 12, 26, 53, 56, 60, 64, 69, 72
higher aspects 44, 47, 72
higher Self 9, 10, 44
higher unconscious 8, 9, 13, 25
Hinkle, Beatrice 20
husband 23, 30, 37, 43, 51, 61, 63
Huxley, Laura 63
Huxley, Aldous 63

I

I and Thou 65
ideal vi, 12, 38, 41, 47, 48, 51, 59, 64, 74, 79
idealism 53
identification 7-8, 10, 22, 44, 46, 50, 67
identifying 44
identity 33, 46, 70
illumination 46
illusion 48, 56

image   37-38, 47-48, 51, 65, 68, 83, 84
impression   48
incentive   39
individuality   33
inferiority   39, 53, 62, 71
initiative   15, 36
inspiration   v, 5, 9, 46, 55
integrated   39, 68, 70, 72
integration   22, 30, 31, 37, 39-40, 47, 50, 52, 60, 61, 68, 72-74
internal   26, 41, 42
introverts, introversion   41-42, 80
inversion   30, 38
invocation   46

J

Joan of Arc   44
Jung, C.G.   2, 13, 20, 31, 38, 79

K

Keyserling, Hermann   16, 18, 21, 38, 54, 59, 79
knowledge   1, 5, 9, 35, 62, 64

L

levels   vi, 7, 13-14, 25, 27-28, 31, 33, 36, 49, 50, 54, 55, 58-60, 79
limitations   39, 45, 74
listening   46-47
Lombard, Catherine Ann   iii, 3-4, 75, 76
love   vi, 28, 33, 36, 40, 43, 48, 52, 58-61, 65, 67-68, 71
lower aspects   2, 47

M

Maeder, Alphonse   2, 16, 20
marriage   iv, 1, 3, 4, 18, 21, 23-25, 28, 35-36, 45, 51, 53-55, 58-59, 62, 70, 72, 76
masculine   vi, 14-17, 29, 38-40, 43, 69-71, 74, 78
Masculine Principle, The Feminine Principle, and Humanistic Medicine,The   15-16
masculine principle   15, 70
matriarchy   37
maturity   7, 9, 66
meditation   18, 46, 66
mental   8, 13, 14, 28, 30, 33, 35-36, 42, 43, 50, 60, 61
methods   ii, 46-47
middle unconscious   8
mother   7, 23, 37, 43, 45, 51, 53, 58, 62, 68, 69, 79
multiplicity   vi, 25, 55, 61, 65

N

Nightingale, Florence   44
Novalis   53

O

order   6, 16, 30, 36, 64, 66, 68, 80

P

Palombi, Ida   83, 84
parent   12, 23, 37, 48, 72, 79, 80
parity   69
Pascoli, Giovanni   44
passive   41-42, 71, 78
patriarchy   37
personalities, personality   13, 29, 35-36, 63, 44, 45, 47, 63-65, 70-72

physical   13-14, 28-29, 33, 35-36, 40, 50, 52, 57-60, 65, 70, 78, 80-81
planes   35
Plato   21
polarity, polarities   12, 14, 16, 29-31, 40, 43, 47, 57, 68, 71, 78-80
positivism   5
possibilities   11, 24, 40, 56, 68
prayer   46
prejudices   69
projection   44, 51
psychosynthesis   i, iv, v, vi, 1-2, 4-10, 12, 14, 17-20, 22-23, 25-28, 30-34, 37, 38, 42, 44-49, 51, 55-56, 58, 60, 64-66, 68, 72-78, 84

Q

qualities   7, 15-16, 31, 39, 44-45, 49, 61, 64, 72, 74

R

Rasponi, Contessa Gabriella Spalletti   4, 44
regulation   26, 47
relationship   iv, 2, 10-11, 18, 23, 25, 28, 31-34, 37, 40, 41, 47, 50-51, 53, 63, 67, 72, 78, 81, 83
Remen, Rachel Naomi, MD   15
repressed   36, 63
respect   vi, 4, 8, 31, 47, 48, 66, 69, 72
responsibility   36
right   2, 3, 13, 39, 47, 52-53, 57-58, 66, 68-69, 71, 83

Roberto Assagioli – The Life and Work of the Founder of Psychosynthesis   4
roles   5, 12, 14, 31, 43, 68-69, 71, 74, 81

S

Sand, George   70
self   7-12, 22, 25, 26, 33, 37, 39-41, 43-44, 51-53, 56, 58, 62, 71, 84
Servan-Schreiber, Claude   12, 14, 76, 84
sex   29, 39, 40, 44-45, 48-49, 51-52, 69-70, 72
Shen, Lijuan   81
single   11, 20, 36, 39, 40
son   vii, 3, 18, 23, 63, 83
Sorokin, Pitirim   52
spirit   5, 39, 47, 64
spiritual   4, 8-10, 13, 17, 24, 26, 28, 33, 34, 41, 43, 46-47, 50, 56, 58, 60, 61, 68
spouse   24, 26-27, 48, 63, 64, 69
stability   26, 56
stages   vi, 7, 22, 34, 50, 66, 67
step   5, 11, 17, 34, 68
stereotypes   69
subconscious   48
subpersonalities   7, 25-26, 55, 63, 65
superconscious   46, 47
suppress   38-39
synthesis   vi, 7, 10, 12, 16, 23, 25, 32-34, 40, 46, 47, 58, 66, 71, 76, 78, 84

T

Tagore, Rabindranath   20
task   27, 33, 41, 48, 51, 68, 74

techniques 47, 73
tendencies 11, 12, 14, 26, 29, 42, 48, 65, 79, 81
tolerate 27, 54
traits 39, 53, 81
transmute 47
transpersonal Self 25
trauma iv
triangular 40
triangularity 40
type 27-30, 42, 44, 61, 63, 78
typological 29, 31, 41, 64

U

unconscious 8-9, 13, 25, 35, 37-39, 50, 53, 69
union 16, 28, 33-36, 46, 65, 80
universal Self 9, 46

V

value 10, 12, 26, 43, 45, 55, 58, 68, 71, 73
vocation 68

W

Way of All Women, The 21
wife iii, 3, 18, 23, 30, 43, 51, 61, 63-64, 66, 68, 82
Wild and Free Creature, A 4
wrong 52, 57-58

Y

yang vi, 16, 79-81
yin vi, 16, 79-81
yoga 5, 9
You Are Not the Target 63

ABOUT THE AUTHORS

Roberto Assagioli, MD (1888-1974) was born in Venice and lived his entire life in Italy. He was a psychiatrist, psychotherapist, teacher, lecturer and writer, among other things. He was among the fist Italians to study Freudian psychoanalysis, and along with C.G. Jung he was among the first to leave the psychoanalytic movement to develop his own framework for psychological and spiritual work. His psychosynthesis, an original synthetic framework for understanding and fostering human understanding, healing, and development, was first presented in 1928 and is now used worldwide in coaching, education, medicine, psychotherapy, organizational development and other fields of endeavor by thousands of people who have taken the training in this framework and used the methods of psychosynthesis. Assagioli founded the Institute of Psychosynthesis in Florence, Italy, and inspired the founding of Sundial House Meditation Centre in the UK, Meditation Mount in Ojai CA in the USA, and The School for Esoteric Studies in the USA. He was an associate of Alice Bailey and produced much material under the auspices of The Arcane School. He was the author of numerous paper, articles, and pamphlets as well as the books *Psychosynthesis: A Manual of Principles and Techniques*; *The Act of Will*; and *Transpersonal Development*.

Piero Ferrucci is an Italian philosopher, teacher, psychotherapist and writer who was a direct student of Roberto Assagioli. He is the author of *What We May Be: Techniques for Psychological and Spiritual Growth Through Psychosynthesis*; *The Power of Kindness: The Unexpected Benefits of Leading a Compassionate Life*; *Your Inner Will: Finding Personal Strength in Critical Times*; and other books and articles. He lives in Italy.

Jan Kuniholm is an American philosopher, writer and editor. He served the Association for the Advancement of Psychosynthesis in numerous capacities, including Co-chair, from 2004-2018; and was founder and original editor of the online journal *Psychosynthesis Quarterly*. He was editor of the book *Sharing Wellness,* a collection of classic articles on psychosynthesis. He has written several papers and articles, and through his imprint Cheshire Cat Books has published books related to psychosynthesis. For some years he has worked with others to bring more of Roberto Assagioli's Italian writings to an English-speaking audience. He lives in Massachusetts, USA.

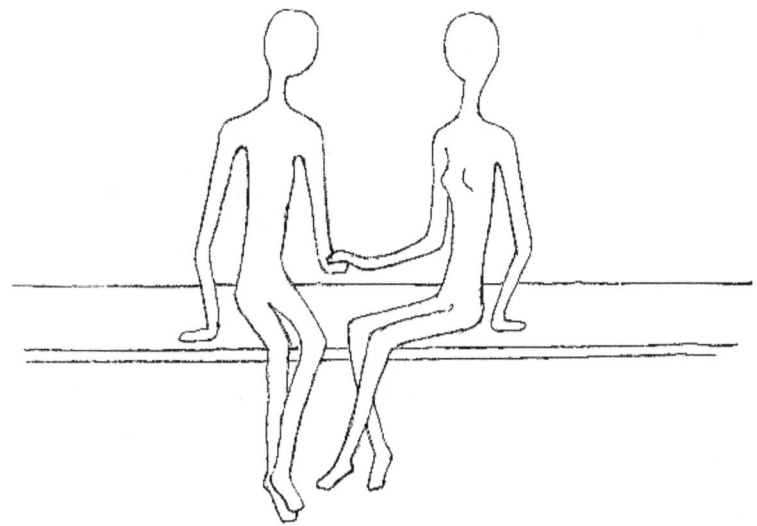

Drawing by Bonney Kuniholm

www.ingramcontent.com/pod-product-compliance
Lightning Source LLC
Chambersburg PA
CBHW020301030426
42336CB00010B/856